S

DATE DUE

JUN 2 2 2017	
APR 2 4 2019	

Stonecutte

Book design: Mark Van Bakel
Cover design: Wayne Van Sickle and George Roth (Polygon
Design Limited)
Chief Editor: Diane Aves
Front cover photograph - Opeongo Lake: Wayne Van Sickle

Back cover photographs -Canoe: Wayne Van Sickle
Moose: Chris Boettger
Fall colours: Todd Carnahan
Author: Todd Carnahan
Additional photography: as indicated beside each image

Published by
Stonecutter Press
212 Arthur Street South
Elmira, Ontario
Canada
N3B 2P1
(519) 669-2374
Email: stonecut@hotmail.com
Website: www.algonquinbooks.cjb.net

Canadian Cataloguing in Publication Data

Van Sickle, Wayne, 1971-
Algonquin Park Visitor's Guide

ISBN 0-9684005-1-5

1. Algonquin Provincial Park (Ont.)—Guidebooks.
I. Title.

FC3065.A65V33 1999   917.13'147   C99-900970-2
F1059.A4V33   1999

ACKNOWLEDGEMENTS

Thank you to my parents,
Susan and Barry.

There is no purer love on Earth
than that which you show me daily;
you are a part of everything I do.

The creation of this book could not have been accomplished in isolation. I would especially like to acknowledge the contributions of the following people:

Marja Sepers, Renee Gorrell, Mark van Bakel, Val Kalnins, Judy Ruan.

Pat Tozer and everyone at the Friends of Algonquin Park. Ron Tozer reviewed large portions of the manuscript for factual accuracy. Dan Strickland's vast body of writings provided me with fantastic introductions to many aspects of the Park; he also painstakingly reviewed the Gray Jay chapter. Doug Currie from the Royal Ontario Museum reviewed my writings on the Black Fly.

The art chapter was among the most enjoyable parts of the project. René Brunet from Wildlife Art Int, greatly assisted my exploration of the art world and steered me toward valuable resources and contacts. Dwayne Harty provided vivid answers to many of my questions regarding Tom Thomson's art. Conversations with Robert Bateman and Chris Bacon helped me gain insight into the artistic process. David Huff at the Tom Thomson Memorial Gallery reviewed and fine-tuned my writings on Tom Thomson. Tony Sepers was a helpful resource and continues to help my understanding of the art world grow.

Andrew Mills, Chris Boettger, Bob Stronach from Algonquin Outfitters, Debbie Dunn, Rich Swift at Algonquin Outfitters, Swift Canoe and Kayak: it is a pleasure to paddle your boats, "G" at MW Continuum Co, Janice from ORCA and Joseph Agnew from the CRCA, Sven Miglin at the Portage Store, Deb Gorgerat, Diane Aves, Dee Dee Milner, John Wall, Diane Van Sickle, Karen Sepers, Mary Jaroszynski, Kathy Cummings, Vivian Pukarowski,

For
Calvin Van Sickle
(1911 - 1998)

CONTENTS

══ LOCATION MAP ══

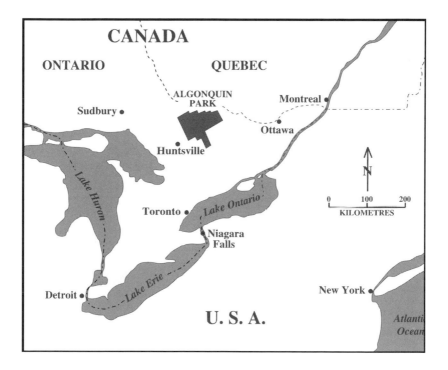

From Toronto:

Algonquin Park's Highway 60 Corridor is roughly three hours by automobile:

- Take Highway 400 North toward Barrie.
- Follow the signs to Highway 11 and North Bay.
- Near Huntsville, take Highway 60 East and follow it into Algonquin Park.

From Ottawa:

Algonquin Park's Highway 60 Corridor is roughly three and one-half hours by automobile:

- Take Highway 417 West out of Ottawa.
- Then take Highway 17 West.
- Follow the signs to Renfrew and Highway 60.
- Follow Higway 60 West through Eganville and Barry's Bay and into Algonquin Park.

1

Wayne Van Sickle

INTRODUCTION

Algonquin Park is Ontario's oldest and most famous Provincial Park. It is a Canadian treasure and an international legend. Its rugged landscape is blanketed in both coniferous and deciduous forests, and is dotted with 2,456 lakes. Rocky shorelines are its trademark. For visitors arriving from each of the four corners of the world, it is a place to experience Canada's wide-open spaces and encounter its abundant wildlife. The Park is home to roughly 2,500 moose, 30,000 beavers, 2,000 black bears and 300 wolves. Amazingly, it lies only a day's drive from the most densely populated region of Canada. For many residents of Southern Ontario, Algonquin is a refuge, a place to disengage temporarily from a fast paced world, and unwind beneath the brilliant stars of the North Sky. Algonquin is among the world's premiere canoe destinations. It is also a fabulous destination to enjoy long distance and day hiking, bicycling, cross-country skiing, dogsledding, snowshoeing, photography, art, bird watching, fishing, fine dining and many other activities.

The Park is massive. At 7,725 km^2, it is larger than Banff National Park in the Rocky Mountains. It is also larger than the entire province of Prince Edward Island. It is impossible to see it all in one visit; in fact, the bulk of the Park can be accessed only by canoe or by foot. Algonquin receives over 400,000 visitors each year. Many are day visitors, but over 100,000 people stay an average of four days in one of the Park's many campgrounds. Others stay at one of three private lodges located in the Park, while the most adventurous set out into the vast Park Interior by way of 29 access points located throughout the Park. These visitors take only what they can carry on their backs, or in their canoes, and stay nightly at one of 1500 Interior campsites, not accessible by any road. These campsites consist of a fire pit, a clearing for a tent and a privy.

The area found along Highway 60, known as the Parkway Corridor, is the most frequently visited part of the Park. It is a spectacularly beautiful region, which is also home to the bulk of the Park's services and facilities. Day hiking trails, campgrounds, museums, outfitters, lodges and shops are situated between the many scenic lakes found along the paved highway. As the number of visitors to the Parkway Corridor rises, there is a growing interest in the more remote parts of the Park. There are three additional regions of the Park where some development has occurred, namely Algonquin South, the East Side and the North Side. Each has a distinct feel to them, and although none has a range of services comparable to that of the Corridor, each has a campground, trails, and associated outfitters. In terms of travel time, the four regions are located quite some distance from each other. Most visitors confine their stay to one area.

There is good reason for the mystique surrounding Algonquin Park. Its deep blue lakes, expansive forests and wild animals each contribute to its splendour. Those who come to visit, whether it is for a brief afternoon picnic, or a two-week canoe trip, are truly fortunate.

As the late Ralph Bice, "the grand old man of Algonquin", who was recently honoured with the renaming of his favourite lake in his name, once said, "Anyone who has been to Algonquin Park will be disappointed when they get to heaven".

I first visited Algonquin Park in my early teens. My family drove to the Park for an afternoon of hiking and posing for family portraits. No photographs resulted from that day because the camera was improperly loaded, but the rugged Algonquin landscape was clearly imprinted in my mind's eye. The Park became a regular haunt of mine as I approached the age of twenty. The call of the loon, the sound of the wind whistling through the pine trees and the smell of wild raspberries brought me back again and again. Numerous solo journeys into the Park's Interior served as rites of passage into manhood, and helped to build my character and forge self-confidence. Algonquin was a great friend to me throughout those years, but, at the time, I had little appreciation for just how unique a place it was.

In my early twenties, I was consumed by the desire to see the world. As opportunities presented themselves, I left Ontario to explore the farthest reaches of North America, and to cross the Atlantic for adventures in faraway lands. Within a few short years I had set foot on four continents and had seen some of the wildest and most awe-inspiring places the world has to offer. As I roamed farther and farther away, my thoughts increasingly returned to Algonquin.

One of the most "Canadian" of all tendencies is to confer more value on faraway places than those close by. I decided to become better aquainted with my roots and rediscover Northern Ontario. I can now say, without hesitation, that the great game parks of East Africa have nothing on Algonquin Park. There is no form of travel more elegant than the silent gliding of a canoe through water, no view as breathtaking as that offered from a vantage point high above a sprawling autumn forest painted gold, orange and scarlet, and no wildlife encounter more magical than meeting a bull moose, adorned with a massive rack of antlers, as it steps out of the thick morning mist.

One of the first things I learned when I began the research for my first book on Algonquin Park was that Germans were visiting the Park in increasing numbers each year. Although they comprised a

Wayne Van Sickle

Morning in Algonquin Park

significant percentage of Park visitors, there was no educational literature on Algonquin in their native language. During my travels, I had benefited greatly from the efforts of local people who took the time to share their special places with me, and after being on the receiving end of such efforts for so long, I decided to return the favour. Although I did not speak German and had never written a book, I set about writing an introductory guidebook to the culture, history, wildlife and hiking trails of Algonquin Park for translation into German. My self-published book, *Naturparkführer Algonquin Park Kanada* was well received. I took great pride in knowing that I had contributed something useful to Park visitors. Soon after it was published, I began to receive queries from people who had seen the book and wondered where they could find a copy in English. They sounded genuinely disappointed when I told them it was available only in German. When requests became increasingly frequent, I put pen to paper, or more aptly, fingers to lap top, and adapted and expanded the original manuscript into its present form.

As much as possible, this book is written in a format to make the individual chapters independent. I wanted visitors to be able to find facts and relevant background information on a wide range of topics with efficiency. Some repetition of fact was necessary to achieve this structure.

2

CONCERNS, PRECAUTIONS AND THINGS TO BE AWARE OF

♦ **Poison Ivy:** Found only in the Barron and Lower Petawawa River regions of the Park's East Side (several day's paddle from Highway 60 campgrounds and facilities).

♦ **Snakes:** There are no poisonous snakes in Algonquin Park.

♦ **Berries and Mushrooms:** Some are tasty, others are quite poisonous. Consult an edible plant field guide before consuming.

♦ **Swimming**: Look before you leap! Lake bottoms are full of huge rocks.

♦ **Driving**:
   1. See the *Moose* chapter for information on how to avoid dangerous moose/car collisions.
   2. Rear-end collisions can occur when drivers become distracted by wildlife. Be sure to pull completely onto the shoulder when stopping to view animals.

♦ **Drinking Water:** Lake and stream water should be boiled for at least seven minutes or filtered or treated with iodine tablets. Never drink water taken near an active beaver pond, or from a dark, murky or stagnant source.

♦ **Animals:**
   1. Feeding Park animals leads to road kills and skirmishes with people which can result in human injury or loss of animal life. (Gray Jays and Chipmunks are the exception to this rule and can generally be fed safely).

2. Proper methods of food storage and other special concerns related to bears, moose, and raccoons are discussed in the animal sections.

♦ **Biting Insects:** Although present from late May through August, biting insects are most troublesome from late May until the beginning of July. See the *Black Flies* and *The Four Seasons* sections for avoidance tactics and more details.

♦ **Highway 60 Kilometre Markings:** Locations of Park facilities, lakes and trails are identified by their distance from the West Gate. Small brown signs with kilometre markings appear regularly on hydro poles along the highway.

♦ **Permits:** Permits provide funding for Park services and facilities. They are required for ALL Park use - inquire at either Gate.

♦ **Toilets:** Toilets are located at campgrounds, day hiking trailheads, picnic grounds, the Visitor Centre, the Algonquin Gallery, the Logging Museum and both Park Gates.

♦ **Cited books:** Most cited books are available at the Visitor Centre bookstore. Those marked with an asterisk (*) are published by a non-profit organization called The Friends of Algonquin Park. Many of their publications are priced at under three dollars and can be shipped worldwide by visiting www.algonquinpark.on.ca/publications.html

3

Algonquin Park Museum

THE HISTORY
OF ALGONQUIN
PARK

Ten thousand years ago the area now regarded as Algonquin Provincial Park emerged from the last of four ice ages to grip North America over a period of one million years. Massive sheets of ice, up to 3 km thick, had bulldozed across the land, scraped up the soil and gouged out valleys. A new rugged landscape of small lakes and rocky cliffs appeared. Great forests took root, and life sprang up.

The first humans to appear in this post ice age period were Paleo-Indians. They arrived in the area roughly 1000 years after the last sheets of ice retreated. They and other Native Americans lived a traditional hunting and gathering lifestyle in the Algonquin Park area until the white, European society came to dominate the region. The first European to reach these forests and lakes was Samuel de Champlain, a cartographer commissioned by the French government. Although he briefly surveyed the region in 1605, he concentrated his efforts elsewhere in the New World. The Algonquin Park area remained largely unmapped and inaccessible for the next two hundred years.

The British Empire found itself in a resource-craved state during the opening years of the 1800's. Its war efforts and economy required shipbuilding lumber and timber faster than it could be supplied. Fur hats made from beaver pelts were the rage among the upper class. The Empire looked to the New World. Those able to provide natural resources became rich. Insatiable demand drove suppliers deeper and deeper into the wilderness all across Canada. These new industries spread like wildfire. In fact, at one point, over one-half of the able-bodied men in Canada found employment in the logging trade. Both loggers and trappers had reached the Algonquin Park area by the 1830's and began to extract its resources at an alarming rate. Loggers, living in primitive camps amid the Algonquin wilderness, felled great White Pine trees all winter long. Logs were stockpiled at the edge of frozen lakes to wait for the swollen spring rivers, upon which they would be floated out of the Park to British ships anchored 650 km away at Quebec City.

A few settlers also trickled in, attracted by erroneous reports that the area's soil was fertile. Most left after discovering the truth, but at one point there were 29 farms or villages in what is now recognized as Algonquin Park.

By the late 1800's countless fires had burnt down huge tracts of forest, and over-trapping had caused beaver populations to plummet. The government of Ontario became concerned about the longevity of the region's timber stands, and about the preservation of its rivers and wildlife. The headwaters of five of the Province's major rivers were located in the area, and it was feared that widespread land clearing, from additional settlement, would cause downstream flooding. In 1893, the Ontario Government formed Algonquin Park, naming it after the Algonquin Indian Nation that had inhabited the area for thousands of years. The few remaining settlers were asked to leave, and trapping became regulated. Wildlife numbers rose to healthy levels again. Although many of the Park's once mighty White Pines had already been cut or burnt down, there were other tree species, and logging continued to be the dominant activity in the area after the creation of the Park. J.R. Booth dominated the Algonquin logging industry. In 1896 he built a railroad to transport timber out of the Park. It was reported to have been the busiest railroad in Canada in the early 1900's. It was said that a train went by every twenty minutes! By the early 1900's, Booth employed over 6000 men and operated the largest company, owned by one man, in the world. Quite impressive for a man who left the family farm at the age of 21 and took a job as a carpenter.

The railroad forever changed the culture of Algonquin Park. Prior to its arrival, the Park had been inaccessible to tourists. The train brought adventuresome types north. More and more of them arrived each year, and several luxury hotels and lodges sprang up along the railroad to serve them. Among the people arriving by train was a painter named Tom Thomson who, between 1914 and 1917, painted some of the most important landscapes in Canadian history. In 1936 the Park's Highway was completed and it brought even more people to the Park. Camping and canoeing were the favourite activities of these visitors. They set out in greater numbers each year to enjoy the Park's blue lakes and abundant wildlife. As canoe tripping became increasingly popular throughout the 1950's and 1960's, tensions between the loggers and the recreators grew and festered. Members of the public formed protest groups that called for the protection of Algonquin's forests.

Government studies were undertaken, public meetings were held, and in 1974 the government revealed its Master Plan for the future management of Algonquin Park. It officially became a Multiple-Use Park in which both the economic value of its timber, and its wilderness feel would be protected. All Park land was examined and classed as belonging to one of four categories: 5.7% was deemed a Nature Reserve or Historical Zone, and was given special protection to preserve its unique geography, nature or history; 12% was classed as a Wilderness Zone in which man interferes as little as possible; 4.3% was termed the Development Zone where campgrounds, lodges, and other high impact activities are allowed; the remaining 78% became known as the Recreational/Utilization Zone in which both canoe camping and logging take place. Within this last zone, logging is prohibited along shorelines and canoe portage trails. Algonquin continues to function today as a Multiple-Use Park.

Further Interest

- *A Pictorial History of Algonquin Park** by RonTozer and Dan Strickland, 1995: 85 wonderful photos from the Park Archives including those of pioneer loggers, early rangers, hotels and railway. $1.95
- *Chronology of Algonquin Provincial Park** by Rory MacKay – Park Technical Bulletin #8, 1993. Bare facts and events of the Park in chronological order. $1.50
- *Names of Algonquin: Stories Behind the Lake and Place Names of Algonuin Park** by G.D. Garland, 1993 - Park Technical Bulletin #10: over 420 names, many of which are Native American. $2.50
- *Glimpses of Algonquin Park* by* G.D.Garland: impressions of 32 writers who visited the Park between 1824 and 1987. $7.95
- *Early Days in Algonquin Park* by Otteryn Addison: A history of the Park beginning with the story of its native peoples. $9.95
- *Algonquin Story** by Audrey Saunders: Historical tales gathered at the end of the Park's first 50 years.
- *The John R Booth Story* by* C.F. Coons and the Ontario Ministry of Natural Resources. The story of the great lumber baron who brought the railway to Algonquin Park. 20 pages complimented by great photos. $2.50
- *J.R. Booth: The Life and Times of an Ottawa Lumberking* by John Ross Trinnell, Treehouse Publishing, Ottawa, 1998.
- Booth's Rock Hiking Trail; learn about the man from the trail's guide booklet.

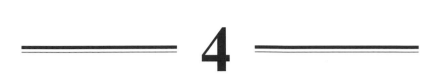

4

DAVID PETER HUNSBERGER
*Dogtooth Violet,*1987
(Trout-lily - *Erythronium americanum)*
Serigraph

THE FOUR SEASONS

I know of nowhere else on the planet where four more distinct seasons occur. The flora and fauna of Algonquin Park undergo profound changes throughout the course of the year. Each season has a unique set of events. The vast majority of Algonquin Park's annual 400, 000 visitors arrive from July to late September. The Algonquin summer is certainly spectacular and deserving of its international reputation, but the more I get to know the Park, the more I crave it in the spring, fall and winter. One of the many benefits of visiting at these times is the greatly reduced probability of encountering other people.

Spring

Spring is the season of renewal, emergence, birth and growth. It is full of sound. The thick ice on Algonquin's lakes begins to thaw in mid-April. It makes the most bizarre noises, some like the popping that can occur when an ice cube is first dropped in a glass of water, others like the cracking of a whip. The strange sounds can be so loud that campers awaken in the night. Loons return from their southern wintering waters a few days after break up, to claim territory on Park lakes. Their mournful wails and undulating yodels are among the most characteristic sounds of the north. As temperatures rise, water trickles over rock faces. Brightly coloured wildflowers laugh into bloom. Shades of yellow, red, pink and white dance upon the forest floor from late April until mid-May, when newly-sprouted leaves in the treetops steal away the sun and darken the forests. Songbirds peep constantly throughout the day, aquatic frogs call out in great numbers and volumes as darkness falls and owls hoot through the night. Spring is the most reliable time of year to experience close-up sightings of moose. In May and June it is not uncommon to see seven or eight moose in one pass of the Park's 56 km highway. The first three weeks of May are the *crème de la crème* of spring. Black Flies arrive by late May and put a serious damper on even the hardiest visitor's ability to enjoy the outdoors. The Park remains relatively empty until Black Fly activity tapers off in late June or early July.

Summer

Mosquitoes, which arrive before the end of the Black Fly outbreak, persist until late July but visitors generally find them manageable. The large biting Deer Flies that are present throughout August are also tolerable. Midsummer temperatures often soar above 25 °C. The abundance of lakes makes swimming one of the season's most popular activities. The Park's 2100 km of canoe routes, 1500 Interior campsites, overnight backpacking trails, day hiking and bicycling trails, restaurants and interpretative services, are heavily used throughout the summer. Numerous seasonal campgrounds and three private lodges within the Park help Algonquin's year-round campground to handle the influx of visitors. Summer is also the time of year when Algonquin's children's camps, some of which have been in operation since the early 1900's, take in close to 2000 girls and boys aged 7 to 16. Over the years, many notable Canadians, including former Prime Minister Pierre Trudeau, TV personality Lorne Green (Bonanza, Lorne Green's New Wilderness) and

Big Trout Lake

Michael Budman and Don Green, the founding partners of Roots Canada, have learned paddling skills and campfire songs from colourful camp counsellors.

Fall

September is many people's favourite time to visit. It is usually bug free. Many services remain in full swing until late October (limited forms of most can be found thereafter), but the number of people using them declines dramatically after the province's children return to school in early September. Warm sweaters keep visitors comfortable in the evening, and sunny afternoons provide the ideal climate for hiking, canoeing and bicycling. Fall's theme is preparation for winter. Plants and animals take action to ensure that they are ready. This preparation is the reason behind the unforgettable display of colour that takes place each fall. Millions of leaves turn from green to golden yellow, orange, red and scarlet. The region's extreme climate, the prominence of the Sugar Maple and the scale upon which the colours can be seen, make this yearly display simply unmatched anywhere. Not to be outdone by the plant world, Algonquin's wildlife attracts plenty of attention as well. Wolves howl back in response to human howling attempts. The sighting of a Bull Moose, whose antlers have grown as large as a piano bench, could very well be the most impressive animal encounter of your lifetime.

Chris Boettger

Winter

Algonquin Park is stunningly beautiful and quiet in the winter. Snow begins to fall in November and hangs heavy on the boughs of conifer trees. Traditionally, lakes are frozen by Christmas. Snow accumulates to depths of up to one metre by midwinter. Temperatures range from sunny daytime highs a few degrees above freezing to nighttime lows approaching -40 °C! Although many Park animals migrate to warmer places or sleep the season away in their dens, others like the fox, moose, otter and wolf remain out and about. Snow records their every movement. Tracks provide a glimpse into their lives in a way that isn't possible at any other time of the year. A winter tracks guidebook and a good imagination can help piece together the events, which led to the pattern left in the snow. Ravens and chickadees are frequently observed and Gray Jays, looking for handouts, often approach visitors. Cross-country skiing is the focus of many peoples' winter visit. Fabulous trails are located along Highway 60, as well as in the Algonquin South Region. Visitors can also set off into the bush on snow shoes or take guided dog sled trips. The Visitor Centre maintains weekend hours throughout the winter and is open daily during the Christmas holidays. A Highway 60 campground, which is open throughout the entire year, serves hearty individuals wishing to spend the night in tents, self-built snow structures, or in canvas-roofed shelters equipped with electrical heaters. The less adventurous will find accommodation and meals at motels and lodges located just outside the Park boundaries.

5

THE BLACK FLY

Black Flies are a global phenomenon. Over 1700 species have been recorded in varying densities in all areas of our planet, save Antarctica and a few dry islands and deserts. They are stout-bodied, hump-backed flies with short broad wings and short legs. Black Flies are easily distinguished from the mosquito, which has long thin legs and a long proboscis snout. Black Flies relentlessly mob warm-blooded creatures, including humans, stealing blood and inflicting painful, itchy bites. While they can be the carriers of serious illness in the tropics, the negative impacts of Canada's approximately 160 species, are largely confined to economic loss for outdoor industries such as farming, timber and recreation. Black Flies have been responsible for the deaths of Canadian cattle, either indirectly by driving to them to tragic stampedes, or directly by taking large amounts of blood from calves. "Man-eating" Black Flies are the main reason for low visitation to Algonquin Park from late May through early July. Although tourists avoid the Park during Black Fly season, insect researchers do not. In fact, Algonquin is somewhat of a Mecca for Black Fly researchers, and it even played host to an International Black Fly Conference held at its Wildlife Research Station in 1962.

Predators and Significance to the Algonquin Ecosystem:
Remarkably, 40 of Ontario's 63 Black Fly species occur in Algonquin Park. This diversity is due partly to a large range of running water habitats. As you might imagine, Black Flies play a major role in the Park's ecosystem. Among the many creatures that feed upon them are dragonflies, damselflies, waterfowl, fish, bats and numerous species of birds. Each spring, birds that have wintered in the tropics fly to Algonquin to nourish their young on the swarms of Black Flies. For many years it has been widely believed that Algonquin's Black Flies are important pollinators of its blueberries. However,

recent studies carried out in Algonquin Park, suggest that although Black Flies visit blueberry flowers to feed on their nectar, they do so without actually pollinating them. (Hunter, 1999).

From Egg to Flying Adult:
Females lay batches of 200 to 500 eggs in streams and rivers or on the partially submerged weeds and rocks at their edges. Many of Ontario's Black Fly species pass winter in the egg-state. When the eggs eventually hatch into larvae, they drift with the current before attaching themselves to rocks, sticks or vegetation in swift-moving water. The larvae filter algae and other organic matter from the water, and shed their skin several times before spinning an underwater cocoon inside of which they eventually transform into winged adults. When the transformation is complete, the insect breaks out of its cocoon, floats to the surface in an air bubble, and takes flight within a few seconds. Black Flies emerge in staggering numbers from Algonquin's watercourses each spring. One researcher who used floating traps to capture adults emerging from Costello Creek, near Opeongo Lake, identified 12 species of Black Flies from May until September, and found that per square meter of stream bottom, over 26, 000 adults emerged! (Hayton, 1979). Mating is a priority for the masses of newly-emerged Black Fly adults. Males often swarm together in their search for females, which are detected visually while in flight. Adult black flies can live up to several weeks.

Adult Diet: Water, Nectar and Blood
In the adult stage of life, all food is of the liquid variety. Black Flies land on plants to consume nectar, which provides nutrients required for flight energy. A diet based on water and nectar suffices for the male, but does not provide the females of most species with enough nutrients for egg production. Females make up the deficit with the blood of birds, mammals and man.

The Mechanics of the Bite:
The biting campaign is carried out exclusively by the females. In fact, the males do not even posses biting anatomy. Each species has its own range of acceptable "blood donors". One species is so highly selective that it is reported to take blood exclusively from the Common Loon. Only three of the Park's 40 Black Fly species are considered to be serious pests to humans *(Simulium venustum, Simulium truncatum, Prosimulium mixtum)*. Black Flies belong to a group of

insects known as "pool-feeders". Unlike mosquitoes, the Black Fly is not built to pierce the skin directly with its bloodsucking device. Instead it creates a wound, waits for it to fill with blood and then slurps it up. The biting process can be viewed in several steps:

1) Tiny teeth and hairs grip the skin and pull it taut.
2) A primary incision is made by the snipping action of the insect's biting apparatus, which includes jaw-like mandibles lined with rows of fine teeth.
3) The wound is deepened to a depth of approximately 0.4 mm.
4) Blood flowing into the wound is sampled for desirability.
5) Saliva, containing anti-clotting agents, is injected into the wound to prevent the blood from clotting in the wound and inside the insect's mouth. The saliva is also thought to contain a substance which later aids in digestion.
6) Sucked-up blood is "pumped" into the stomach with powerful muscles located in the insect's head. When full, a Black Fly can be up to twice its normal size.
7) The mouthparts (some of which are barbed) are removed from the host by simple pulling and tugging.

Once in the stomach, the blood quickly forms a semi-solid lump. Digestion takes approximately five to seven days and the female lays her eggs shortly thereafter. The females of many species lay more than one batch of eggs and therefore go looking for blood again.

How Do They Find Us?
Black Flies collect sensory information with their eyes, antennae and sensilla located on their legs and mouth. They are attracted to human odours and also respond to visual cues such as colour, movement and silhouetted shapes. Their ability to detect the carbon dioxide that we exhale also plays a role. The order in which they react to these stimuli and the relative priority placed on each one are not yet fully understood.

The Bloody Aftermath
The anti-coagulant injected into the wound can cause it to continue bleeding even after the insect has finished dining. Bites may or may not be painful at the time, and although Black Flies can take over 5 minutes to "fill up" on our blood, we often do not realize that we have been bitten until after they have flown away. The red and

swollen lesion that usually develops at the bite can last up to 72 hours and remain itchy for up to seven days. Some relief can be obtained by applying calamine lotion, zinc oxide or "after bite" insect preparations to the skin. Biting can also cause swelling of lymph glands and some people inflict secondary infections on themselves by scratching the bites. The vast majority of people experience nothing more than swollen, itchy welts; however, just as some people can have severe allergic reactions to wasp stings, others can be highly sensitive to Black Fly bites and experience a more generalized anaphylactic reaction. Many other kinds of mild to severe reactions can be experienced in rare cases. Most of these are short-lived, such as Black Fly Fever, in which an individual who has received many bites experiences flu-like symptoms, but others can be chronic.

Personal Protection

Black Flies are much more than just a minor annoyance and can seriously impair the enjoyment of a trip to the Park. Unfortunately, many people are either unaware of them or dismiss their importance in the planning stages of their trip. If at all possible, you should plan your visit around their outbreak, but if that isn't possible, then the following will help reduce the Black Fly problem:

1) Black Flies are claustrophobic. Generally they do not bite indoors, or in any type of enclosure (including cars and tents).
2) Biting is more pronounced in the early morning, late afternoon and early evening. (also on warm overcast days, or when a storm is approaching).
3) Biting is more prevalent in "the bush" than in open areas.
4) Clothing provides good protection: wear long-sleeve shirts (keep the fronts and cuffs tightly closed - zippers are preferable to buttons), tuck trousers into socks and wear a hat.
5) Select outdoor clothing and equipment by colour: dark colours, such as blue, black red, brown, purple, maroon, and dark green are more attractive to Black Flies than light colours, such as white, yellow, light grey or green. Matte surfaces, and those reflecting less light, are also more attractive than glossy, reflective surfaces.
6) Black Flies do not deal well with smoke or a moderate wind: choose the windiest places for rest areas or campsites (often found on points or islands) and build a campfire if appropriate.

7) Repellants containing DEET (N, N-dimethyl-m-toluamide), 2-ethyl-1, 3-hexanediol, oil of citronella or dimethyl phthalate provide good protection. The most effective ones are those with higher concentrations of the active ingredients. Apply them thinly and evenly, paying special attention to exposed areas (back of neck, along the hairline, forehead, temple, face, wrists, back of hands and ankles). Always read the directions and keep the repellant out of your eyes, mouth and nose. Repellant applied to clothing can have a long-lasting effect but can also cause fabric breakdown. Specially made "bug jackets" which are impregnated with repellants or have meshed facial areas also provide protection.

*Never apply DEET repellants to the skin of infants.

Further Interest

- *Insects of Algonquin Provincial Park** by Steve Marshall. Over 200 amazingly detailed colour photos accompany an introduction to the diverse insect world of the Park. 48 pages, $2.95

- *The Dragonflies and Damselflies of Algonquin Provincial Park** by Matt Holder. Information and illustrations concerning 35 of the Park's most common species. Park Technical Bulletin # 11, 40 pages. $2.95

6

Sugar Maple (Acer saccharum) leaves

FALL COLOURS

Each fall, deciduous trees throughout the Park undergo stunning transformations of colour. Green gives way to yellow, gold, orange, red and even scarlet. The Sugar Maple tree experiences the most profound changes. Evergreen trees, which ring the shores of Algonquin's lakes, offset the deep blue lake water below and the bright multi-coloured hardwood hills rising above. Breathtaking arrangements await the visitor around every bend.

When does this occur?
Fluctuations in temperature cause the timing of this event to vary slightly from year to year. However, several different tree species undergo colour transformations and visitors can generally expect striking views from mid-September to late October. The most intense colour, often referred to as the "the peak", usually occurs during the last week of September or the first week of October, when Sugar Maple trees turn bright scarlet. Poplar and Red Oak trees continue to provide colourful views throughout October.

Where are the best places to view the colours?
- The Observation Deck of the Visitor Centre (km 43)
- Hardwood Lookout Trail (km 13.8)- Post 9
- Lookout Trail (km 39.7) - Post 4
- Brewer Lake (km 48.6)
- Booth's Rock Trail - (8 km south at km 40.3) Posts 7 and 8
- Centennial Ridges Trail (km 37.6) - virtually any of the trail's lookout points provide stunning views.
- Whiskey Rapids Trail (km 7.2)

Why do the leaves change colour?
At any given time, the colour of a leaf is determined by the dominant pigment found within it. Spring and summer leaves contain green, yellow and orange pigments, but the green pigment (chlorophyll) is usually present in sufficient quantities to overpower the others and effect the green appearance we are so used to. Green gives way to yellow and orange in the fall because levels of chlorophyll decrease to the point where it is no longer dominant. The scarlet colour seen later in Sugar Maple leaves is the result of a new pigment manufactured just before the leaves fall off the trecs.

Leaves contain magnesium, nitrogen, calcium, potassium and other important minerals and nutrients originally absorbed from the soil by way of the tree's roots. They make use of some of these substances in the manufacture of chlorophyll. Chlorophyll captures the energy of the sun, and drives the process whereby leaves produce the basic building blocks of a tree. The production process does not run year round. The reduction of light quality and water availability that occurs as the growing season tapers off, signal the tree to begin transferring the minerals and nutrients from its leaves, to the trunk and branches for winter storage. As these substances depart, leaves are no longer able to manufacture chlorophyll. As the existing chlorophyll breaks down, the yellow and orange pigments that were always present, but in the minority, become dominant and give the leaves new colours.

After the leaves turn golden yellow, Sugar Maple trees manufacture a bright scarlet pigment in order to protect the leaves from the cold. This protection allows the salvage process to continue longer than would otherwise be possible. Eventually the cold and the ultraviolet rays of the sun cause the leaves to turn brown and fall off the tree.

Although European Sycamores, and many other trees around the world, treat people to bright fall colours, none produce colours as bright as the North American Sugar Maple. Its transformations are particularly brilliant due to the high content of sugar within its leaves, and the extreme climate, which causes it to manufacture more of the scarlet pigment than its counterparts in more moderate climates.

Further Interest
- The Dorset Scenic Tower is a 100-foot (30 m) structure, which overlooks the expansive forests surrounding beautiful Lake of Bays. The 128-step climb to the top can be a bit unnerving, but the view is more than worth it – especially during the peak of the fall colours. Take Highway 60 west (toward Huntsville) from the Park's West Gate. Follow it for approximately 20 km, then turn left on Highway 35. Dorset Scenic Tower Road is on the right approx. 15 km later. A small parking fee applies.
- Those wishing to co-ordinate their visit to the Park with the peak of the fall colours can receive updates on the state of the colour changes and the approach of the peak from the Algonquin Park Information Office.

7

Renee Gorrell

PARK
ACTIVITIES

An incredibly wide range of physical, educational and leisure activities await Park visitors. There are many things to do in each of the four seasons. Equipment for activities may be rented or purchased from several Park Outfitters, many of whom also arrange guiding services. See the *Outfitting Chart* for details.

Canoeing:

Algonquin Park is one of the world's most famous canoe destinations. More than 2400 lakes, 2100 km of routes, 1500 Interior campsites, varied wildlife and rugged scenery make any canoe experience unforgettable. The vast majority of the Park's canoeing territory is comprised of lakes or rivers, with few rapids and little discernible flow of water. This "flatwater" territory means that an afternoon of canoeing, as well as a weeklong trip, is a realistic option for most able-bodied visitors. Virtually anyone can learn to operate a canoe in a day, although its tipsy nature and difficulty to control in wind can lead to dangerous situations for those who do not take the time to properly learn the basics. Consult the *Learning Safe Canoe Operation* section toward the back of this book for more information on how to learn the necessary skills.

- **Renting** – Canoes, paddles and life jackets can be rented from several outfitters located inside the Park or close to it. Some provide roof racks, enabling clients to transport the canoes on their own vehicles, while others deliver/pick-up canoes to customers, paying by credit card, at Park Campgrounds. The Portage Store on Canoe Lake, Opeongo Algonquin Store on Opeongo Lake and Bartlett Lodge on Cache Lake, rent canoes and are located directly on the water, making it possible to start canoeing immediately.

- **Day Trips** - Each Park campground is located on the shore of a picturesque lake suitable for canoeing. Visitors who pack themselves a lunch will have no trouble amusing themselves for hours on end as they paddle the shorelines or canoe out to explore islands. There are countless other areas to explore including Canoe Lake, the inspiration for many of the paintings of the late Tom Thomson, and the Opeongo Lake / Costello Creek area where day trippers can visit both the Park's largest lake as well as one of its hottest spots for encountering wildlife. Both areas have on-site canoe rental agents; see the *Day Trips* section for more information.

- **Multi-Day Trips** - On calm days, participants paddle, swim and enjoy rugged scenery by day, and relax under the stars by blazing campfires in the evening. On foul weather days, they work hard to stay warm, dry, safe and well fed. Trippers stay at basic lakeshore campsites, which are not accessible by road. Many visitors purchase a completely outfitted and guided trip from an Outfitter/Professional Guide who plans and leads the trip, as well as provides all the necessary food and equipment. However, many others travel independent of a guide. Independent trippers need to be fully self-sufficient. They should have prior camping and canoeing experience, be able to read maps, contend with adverse weather conditions and know how to animal-proof their food. They must carry all the necessary gear, including tents, cook stoves and sleeping bags, plan their own route and register it with the Park beforehand. All required gear, including pre-packed food, may be obtained from Park Outfitters. See the *Trip Journals* section for a personal account of an incredible ten-day autumn canoe trip. Suggestions for those wishing to plan their own canoe trip can be found in the *Planning an Interior Trip* section.

Whitewater Canoeing and Kayaking:
Algonquin is a flatwater destination largely free of rapids and rivers that provide whitewater opportunities. The only exception is the Petawawa River flowing downstream from Cedar Lake in the northern reaches of the Park. For more information on this river, consult the *Petawawa River Whitewater Guide**. Good whitewater rivers are located just outside Park Boundaries - see
The Madawaska River/Opeongo River Whitewater Guide* for details.

Flatwater Kayaking:
Any multi-day water trip is bound to include significant travel over land between lakes. Kayaks are more difficult to carry on land than canoes are. Algonquin is not traditionally known as a kayaking destination. However, the Park's larger lakes can be enjoyable destinations for flatwater, sea and recreational kayaking. Opeongo Lake is the Park's largest lake, and provides limited multi-day opportunities.

Day-Hiking Trails:
The 14 day-hiking trails located along Highway 60 were designed to provide visitors with a wide variety of experiences. Some lead to fabulous lookout points, or historically or naturally significant areas, while others were specifically designed for encountering wildlife. The trails themselves range from being almost entirely flat to quite steep. The shortest can be hiked in under an hour, while the

Wayne Van Sickle

There are 14 day hiking trails found along Highway 60.

longest requires over six hours. Chief Park Naturalist Dan Strickland has written an educational booklet for each trail pertaining to the natural and human history of the area. Each trail's guide booklet is designed to be read during the walk and can be picked up free of charge at the trailhead. (Please deposit them in the boxes located at the end of the trail so that others may enjoy their use). The *Highway 60 Trail Comparisons and Rankings Chart* ranks the trails with respect to length, difficulty, wildlife potential and the beauty of the lookout point(s). The *Day Hiking Trails* section provides quick overviews, highlights and photos of each trail. The average hiking time listed for each trail was calculated for adults walking at a steady pace. Visitors should add to that time if they plan on taking lengthy breaks at the lookout points or if they will be hiking with children. Day hiking trails are also located in Algonquin South, on the Park's East Side and on its North Side – see the *Services* section for details.

Overnight Backpacking:
Three Overnight Backpacking Trails provide multi-day hiking opportunities ranging from a weekend to a full week. The Western Uplands Backpacking Trail, located at km 3, contains three hiking loops of 32, 55 and 71 km, while The Highland Backpacking Trail, located at km 29.7, provides loops of 19 and 35 km. The Eastern

Taking a well earned break along the Highland Backpacking Trail

Pines Backpacking Trail, located on the Park's more remote East Side, contains loops of 6 km and 14.8 km. Accommodation on all three trails is at basic lakeshore campsites consisting of a fire pit, a tent clearing and a pit toilet. Hikers must be self-sufficient, carry everything they need, and register their route with Park staff beforehand. An account of one of my memorable backpacking adventures is included in the *Trip Journal* section of this book. For more information on planning your own backpacking adventure, consult the *Planning an Interior Trip* section.

Bicycling:
The Minnesing Trail, for mountain biking, is located at km 23 on Highway 60. It is rated as moderate and contains loops of 4.7 km, 10.1 km, 17.1 km and 23.4 km in length. A flatter and less technical trail suitable for bicyclists of all ages is found between Mew Lake and Rock Lake Campgrounds. It is 10 km long and is built upon an old railway line. A 5 km mountain biking trail is found in Algonquin South area – see the *Services* section for details.

Day trips can be fun for everyone, but only those with considerable winter camping experience should plan overnight snowshoeing trips.

Snowshoeing:
Park visitors can set out for day trips from virtually anywhere along the Park Highway (except for the cross-country ski trails, which are groomed exclusively for skiing) including the day hiking trails. For experienced individuals wanting an overnight adventure, options include:

- A special 8 km trail starting from the Minnesing Trail parking lot and carrying on across Canisbay Lake.
- The 10 km bicycle trail between Mew Lake and Rock Lake.
- Any of the Overnight Backpacking Trails (steep inclines can present challenges).

Sufficient snow is usually present between late December to early March. Ice surfaces, especially those around creek mouths, should be tested early and late in the season for safety.

Cross-Country Skiing:
The skiing season generally runs from late December to mid-March. Three trails are located along Highway 60. They are packed and groomed throughout the winter. Along its length, each has shelters

containing emergency rations of first aid equipment, duct tape, chocolate bars and sleeping blankets. Some are heated.

- The Fen Lake Trail starts at the West gate and offers loops of 1.25 km, 5.2 km and 13 km in length.
- The Minnesing Trail at km 23 contains several loops ranging from 4.7 km to 23.4 km in length.
- The Leaf Lake Trail at km 53.9 contains several loops ranging from 5 to 7 km in length.

Eighty kilometres of first rate trails are also maintained in the Algonquin South Region; see the *Services* chapter for details.

Further Interest:
- *Algonquin Provincial Park in Winter:* a free pamphlet providing an overview of winter activities. Included are great maps of cross-country ski trails as well as a look at snowshoeing, dogsledding and winter camping. Contact the Park Information Office for a copy.

Guided Dog Sledding:

Algonquin is one of Canada's hotbeds of dog sled activity. Numerous dog sledding companies are based in the region. Guides teach clients to drive their own team of three to six dogs and then lead them on adventures lasting a few hours, a few days or the better part of a week. Longer trips include overnight accommodation in rustic cabins or canvas-walled tents in or near the Park, or at lodges outside the Park. Trips involve plenty of work and exercise; clients are involved as much as possible in camp duties, including feeding and managing the dogs. The season usually runs from December to March. The *Trip Journals* section contains an account of my first dog sledding expedition.

Star Gazing:

Algonquin is located quite some distance away from big city lights. Its dark night sky provides wonderful contrast for viewing thousands of stars, as well as planets, meteor showers and even man-made satellites. Sightings of the Northern Lights (*aurora borealis)* are not uncommon.

Further interest:
- *Night Watch* by Terrance Dickinson (Firefly 1998): the standard reference guide for novices.

Wayne Van Sickle

Algonquin Park has a solid reputation as being one of the easiest places in the world to encounter moose in the wild.

Animal Viewing:

Algonquin Park is one of the easiest places in North America to encounter wild animals such as moose, beaver, loons, foxes, and wolves. Although Park visitors may see or hear these animals virtually anywhere, at any time, there are a number of things that can be done to increase the odds of a sighting. By far the most important factor is the time of day. Prime time begins roughly one half hour before sunrise and includes the two or three hours afterwards, while sunset and the few hours sandwiching it rank second. Sun times vary significantly throughout the year - check the *Sun Times Chart* in the back of the book before planning your excursion. Bring along your binoculars for better viewing and a copy of this book so you can read about the animals you encounter. Don't forget to record your sightings in the *Wildlife Sightings Chart* for later reference!

- **By Automobile - "the circuit":** Automobile excursions tend to yield the greatest number of sightings due to the amount of territory covered, as well as the fact that vehicles already pulled off the road alert other visitors to the presence of animals they may have otherwise driven by. For maximum success, I recommend driving the Highway 60 circuit. "The circuit" commences

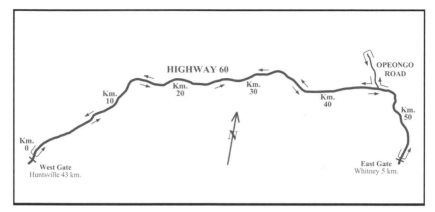

"The Circuit"

at either Park Gate and involves driving along Highway 60, and turning North at Opeongo Road (km 46.3), which drivers follow to its conclusion 6 km later before turning around and carrying on along Highway 60. Drivers turn around in the parking lot at the far Gate, and return along Highway 60 to the Gate from which they started. For best results, repeat the circuit until prime viewing hours end.

Passengers should scan the shoulders of the road continuously for movement or for animals standing still at the edge of the forest. Pay special attention to low-lying wet regions, ponds and smaller lakes. Take a close look along the shoreline of Lake Of Two Rivers (km 32 –35) where loons frequently fish, and at Euclalia Lake (km 39) which I refer to as "Animal Central" because of frequent moose sightings. Check the waters at the junction of Opeongo Road and Highway 60 for the "V"-shaped wake of beaver. Keep your eyes peeled along Opeongo Road. In the past I have had great luck spotting moose, beavers, otters, grouse, Gray Jays, Great Blue Heron and even wolves along the banks of the creek that follows the road. Check for loons in the waters at the road's end, where the creek meets Opeongo Lake.

- **On Foot:** Several day-hiking trails along Highway 60 regularly lead visitors to encounters with moose, beavers, grouse, and other creatures. An early morning or early evening walk may

39

be productive if you choose the right trail. Consult *The Trail Comparisons and Rankings Chart* for a look at the trails with respect to animal potential, hiking time, difficulty.

- **By Canoe:** Waking before sunrise and gliding silently through still waters is the best way to encounter wildlife when camped in the Interior. There is far more animal activity at that time than during the day. Pick a starry night to turn in early, consult the *Sun Times Chart*, and set your alarm for a half-hour before sunrise. Follow your Canoe Routes Map to any bogs, streams or creeks located nearby.

A brief story conveys one final note about animal watching in Algonquin: last summer I had relatives from Calgary visiting who desperately wanted to see a moose. For two straight days, we visited the appropriate places at the best times, but in the end they went home without seeing a thing. The very next day after they had left, I saw three large moose, a beaver and a wolf! There are no guarantees - that's why it's so special when a sighting does occur. If at first you don't succeed, try, try again…

Further Interest:
- *Mammals of Algonquin Provincial Park** by Dan Strickland & Russell J. Rutter. From mice to moose, this 50-page book contains quick overviews of 35 mammals found in the Park as well as great sketches of animal droppings and tracks. Just $1.50!
- *Reptiles and Amphibians of Algonquin Park** by Dan Strickland and Russell J. Rutter. A look at habitats, feeding behaviour and physical features of Park frogs, toads, snakes, turtles and salamanders. 32 pages. $1.00
- The Visitor Centre has a sightings board where visitors record wildlife encounters. It may provide ideas for places to check.

Bird Watching:
Algonquin Park lies in the transition zone between northern coniferous forests and broad-leaved southern hardwood forests and is therefore home to, or a migratory stopping point for birds from both types. Visitors can see true northerners such as the Gray Jay and Spruce Grouse as well as southerners like the Indigo Bunting and Wood Thrush. In all, 266 species of birds have been identified within the Park; 138 are known to breed here. Traditionally hot birding locations include the Spruce Bog Boardwalk (km 42.5), and the

Old Airfield near the Mew Lake Campground (ask campground office staff for directions). During the summer months, Park naturalists conduct public bird watching walks. Birders can enquire with naturalists at the Visitor Centre for detailed information about the latest sightings.

Further interest:
- *The Birds of Algonquin Provincial Park** by Dan Strickland: approximately 100 colour photos accompany 40 pages of information on Algonquin's main bird habitats as well as the biology and ecology of 77 of the most common birds in the Park. The last page in the book lists numerous birding resources on sale at the Visitor Centre bookstore including field guides, bird behaviour guides and bird recording cassettes. $2.95
- *Checklist and Seasonal Status of the Birds of Algonquin Provincial Park** by Ron Tozer: detailed information regarding the first recorded 262 bird species including average and extreme arrival and departure dates, abundance and breeding status. Also recommends 20 great birding locations. Park Technical Bulletin #9. $1.50

Butterfly Watching:
Eighty species of butterflies have been identified within Algonquin Park. This colourful population includes members of the majority of North America's butterfly families. In the summer months, Park naturalists lead walks through prime butterfly territory.

Further Interest:
- *The Butterflies of Algonquin Provincial Park** by Gard W. Otis: a superb 40 page introduction to the lives of Algonquin's 57 most common butterflies; includes 100+ colour photos and lists further publications and organizations related to butterflies. $2.95
- *Checklist of Butterflies of Algonquin Provincial Park** by John D. Reynolds. An annotated list of all butterfly species recorded in the Park, complete with comments on abundance, habitat and flight patterns. Park Technical Bulletin # 1. $0.75

Flora Observation:
Algonquin Park is a fantastic destination to observe and learn about botany. It is home to over 1000 species of plants and another 1000 species of fungi. Scientists and other experts have written a number of inexpensive top quality resources for visitors.

Wayne Van Sickle

"Red Trillium" *(Trillium erectum L)*

Further Interest:

- *Wildflowers of Algonquin Provincial Park** by Dan Strickland and John LeVay: over 55 colour photos compliment informative text about the Park's most common wildflowers, 32 pages. $1.00
- *Mushrooms of Algonquin Provincial Park** by R. Greg Thorn: 75 colour photos help readers learn the major groups and identify the most common species, 32 pages. $2.50
- *Trees of Algonquin Provincial Park**: this 40-page book presents the most common trees in the Park. 150 great colour photos make it easy for anyone to identify species. $2.95
- *Checklist of Bryophytes of Algonquin Provincial Park** Park Technical Bulletin # 2. $0.50
- *Checklist of Vascular Plants of Algonquin Provincial Park**. Park Technical Bulletin # 4. $2.00
- *Checklist of Conspicuous Fungi of Algonquin Park** Park Technical Bulletin # 6. $1.50
- *Checklist of Lichens of Algonquin Provincial Park** Park Technical Bulletin # 7. $0.50

Swimming:

Virtually any lake is good for swimming and most campgrounds have a sandy public beach. Good swimming can also be found at the beaches near the picnic grounds at Lake Of Two Rivers (km 33.8).

42

Fishing:

Algonquin Park offers fine fishing for Lake Trout and Speckled Trout (aka Brook Trout) in the spring. Smallmouth Bass may also be caught in the summer and fall. To protect stocks, fishing is regulated with restrictions on size and number of fish caught, the type of bait used, and time of year. Permits are required. Infractions result in severe penalties. Trout season generally runs from late April until the end of September, while Bass season runs from late June until late November. The *Canoe Routes of Algonquin Map* depicts the location of all of Park lakes.

Further Interest:
- *Fishing in Algonquin Provincial Park** by Dan Strickland. Techniques for catching trout and bass, lake by lake accounting of fish species, present day fisheries management, regulations and descriptions of the yearly species cycles, spawning and growth patterns. $1.95
- *The Incomplete Anglers* by John D. Robbins.* A humorous, semi-fictional account of a 1943 fishing trip in Algonquin Park. $7.95

Picnic Areas:

There are six picnic areas along the Park Highway: Oxtongue River (km 3), Tea Lake Dam (km 8), Canisbay (km 23), Lake of Two Rivers (km 33.8), Lake of Two Rivers East (km 35.4) and Costello Creek (km 46.3). All have public toilets, picnic tables and garbage cans. I prefer Tea Lake Dam, Canisbay and either of the Lake of Two River sites.

Interpretive Program Events:

Algonquin's exceptional Interpretive Program serves as a model for Parks throughout North America. Events occur in the Highway 60 Corridor from late June until early September. Weekly schedules entitled *"This Week in Algonquin"* are posted on bulletin boards found at Park Campgrounds, Offices and Facilities.
- Conducted walks and canoe outings: one to five hour guided outings led by a Park naturalist, which are focussed on specific topics as diverse as wildlife, plants and human history.
- Evening Programs: slide shows and films on Algonquin wildlife and history shown nightly at the Outdoor Theatre (km 35.4). Programs begin at dusk and are held at the Visitor Centre on rainy evenings.

*Algonquin Park is a great place for children. With adequate plan-
ning and proper supervision they can participate in most Park activities. This two year old is pictured on her first overnight canoe
trip. By the age of three and a half she had also walked the Spruce
Bog Boardwalk and the Two Rivers day hiking trails completely
under her own power.*

- Algonquin for Kids: one-hour sessions of nature games and stories for children aged five to twelve and their parents. Programs are held at the Visitor Centre.
- Special Events: *This Week in Algonquin* also lists upcoming special events such as Public Wolf Howls (see *Wolf* section) and Spirit Walks (see *Logging Museum Trail*).

A smaller version of this program operates in the summer in the East Side of Algonquin – See the *Services* section for details.

Horseback Riding

Horseback riding is available along the Highway 60 corridor, in Algonquin South and in Algonquin's East Side.
- Leaf Lake Trail Network (Hwy 60): Cabins located along the more than 50 km of trails may be used for lunch breaks but not for overnight accommodation. Users may camp or stay in their trailer on a large grassy parking lot (complete with vault toilets and a manure bunker), overlooking a lake. The trail is cleared in late July. The parking lot is not sign-posted. Interested parties must contact the information office for reservations and details prior to arrival.
- The over 50 km of spectacular riding trails located in Algonquin South are accessed via an Equestrian Outfitter who also provides trailer parking and guided trail rides for those without their own horses. See Algonquin South in the *Services* chapter.
- The East Side's Lone Creek Riding Trail, which offers day and overnight rides, is described in the East Side section in the *Services* chapter.

8.1

Wayne Van Sickle

DOG SLEDDING TRIP JOURNAL

The following are excerpts from the journals I wrote on my first-ever dog sledding adventure. For five days in early March, I made my home in the most northern reaches of the Interior of Algonquin Park. Under the watchful eye of an experienced guide from Chocpaw Expeditions, I mushed my own team of dogs across frozen lakes and through snowy forests. It was an experience I will not soon forget.

Day 1

I arrived at Expedition Headquarters on a cold March morning and was introduced to the three other clients who had signed up for the trip. Gerhard and Alice were a middle-aged couple from Germany, here for the second year in a row. Donna, a local, worked as a part-time canoe guide in the summer. Over the next five days, each of us would drive our very own sled pulled by a team of four Alaskan sled dogs. Our guide called our attention to the demonstration sled in the middle of the room for an orientation talk. I was nervous about the fact that I had no prior dog sledding experience, but our guide, Sven, assured me that trips were designed with the understanding that most people will have little or no experience.

A fluffy, brown, retired sled dog named Coach helped Sven teach us how to put on and remove the dog harnesses that attached them to the "main line" that ran through the middle of the team. Our prime responsibility as drivers would be to ensure that the main line remained tight at all times. A slack mainline leads to dangerous situations where the rope can become wrapped around a dog's legs. The driver controls the tightness of the mainline by regulating the speed of the sled, by stepping on a sharp-toothed brake located at the back of the sled. Among the many other things we learned were hand signals to communicate states of readiness or the need for assistance over distances greater than earshot.

After the talk, we donned our parkas and set out into the cold to meet our dog teams. Excited barking broke the morning silence as the dogs sensed our approach. There was no doubt about their eagerness. Sven introduced me to my lead pair first. Mitch was a wily veteran, reputed to be among the best lead dogs in the yard. Her partner Hawk, a toffee-coloured dog with a coat lightly dusted with black specks, had recently been promoted up from the rear. My team's rear pair consisted of Zeus and Cola. As the trip progressed I would come to regard Cola as somewhat of a police dog. She watched me closely throughout the entire trip and gave me disapproving glances whenever I slacked off. Zeus was the largest and most friendly dog of the team; he licked my face as I bent forward to look into his beautiful hazel eyes.

We harnessed the dogs and lined the teams up at the trailhead. My team brought up the rear of the group. I stood on the runners at the back of the sled and gazed pensively at the route ahead. I was nervous and sure that I would crumble under the pressure of command or that the dogs would simply refuse to pull me. I readied my team and hoped for the best as the sleds ahead of me began to pull away down the trail. The dogs lurched forward like Olympic sprinters bursting out of the blocks the instant I took my foot off the brake. I felt the wind rush cool across my face and watched the snow move quickly between the runners at my feet. It was a gorgeous moment! No longer nervous, I stood tall knowing that everything was going to be all right. I heard myself shout "Good dogs, that's it", and "Atta girl Mitch". My level of excitement surprised me, and as I glanced around at the white blankets of snow on either side of me and my sled, I felt a little like old Saint Nick mushing his way through a winter wonderland to deliver Christmas presents.

Had Santa travelled overland with a team of dogs, instead of through the sky with a bunch of reindeer, he wouldn't have had a tummy that shook like a bowl full of jelly. It was hard work driving a dog team! I was kept busy applying the brake and helping with the forward motion of the sled. On smaller inclines I kicked alongside like a kid on a skateboard. On larger hills I got completely off to lighten the load for the team, and when confronted with a steep incline, I helped push the sled.

Sled dogs are trained to follow the dog in front of them. Sometimes they get confused when confronted with wide, open space. That's exactly what happened to my team around noon when we came out of the forest and onto a small frozen lake. Sven's lead team had veered to the right shoreline and was dutifully followed by the other teams. But I had let my team fall behind and they weren't sure which way to go. They decided to cross the lake and take the far shoreline. Despite repeated attempts, I couldn't turn them around. Finally, I applied the brake and ground the team to a halt. Before I could even signal for assistance, I spotted Sven running across the lake, calling out to my lead dogs. As soon as Mitch heard Sven, she turned the team and we were off in the direction of the others. Sven told me that Mitch understood the concept of left and right and that if I slowed the team and shouted out "Gee" or "Ha" (the dog-speak equivalents of right and left) that Mitch would turn the team accordingly. Having known plenty of dogs in my days, I had my doubts about this, but I tested it out later that afternoon when the dogs began to head in the wrong direction at a fork in the trail. I stepped on the brake, yelled "Mitch, Ha" and watched in amazement as Mitch, who was on the left side of a directionally-challenged Hawk, jumped straight overtop of him and pulled the team down the right path!

We pulled into Camp 1 around 3 p.m. It consisted of a large canvas tent affixed to a wooden frame in a small clearing in the forest. The 8 x 5 metre structure contained large sleeping platforms and was heated by two wood stoves, which also provided the luxury of stovetop cooking. We chained the dogs up and then split up camp duties. Alice and Gerhard began sawing and chopping wood, Sven and Donna went off in search of additional wood, and I walked down to the lake with a bucket and an axe to fetch some water. A thick layer of ice more than 50 cm deep had formed on the lake by this point in the winter. A hole, kept open by repeated use, had already frozen over since the last expedition had used it the day before. I smashed through the ice with a few axe blows and filled up the buckets. Later on, Alice and I took two large pails of heated water to the dogs. We threw in leftover sandwiches from lunch and let the dogs drink their fill. Zeus was so excited that he plunged into the bucket right up past his eyeballs.

Maintaining the health of the dogs is paramount. We gave the dogs their dinner before preparing a yummy stir-fry for ourselves. By the time we had eaten and washed the dishes it was 8 p.m. and eyes were getting heavy. We took a quick look at the day's journey on the map before settling into our sleeping bags and falling off to sleep. The fires burning in the wood stoves kept it cozy and warm inside the tent, while outside temperatures dipped below $-20°C$.

Day 3
I awoke at 7 a.m. to the golden paste of the sun on the canvas tent wall and the anticipation of a 35 km day, which would take us across three lakes before arrival at the next camp. Our trail had recently been travelled by a pack of wolves. We followed their tracks to the shores of North Tea Lake, which appeared suddenly out of the trees, its vast white flatness stretching as far as our eyes could see. We stuck close to the winding shoreline for most of the journey, occasionally mushing across small bays. It was hard work for the team,

especially when we encountered drifts, which bogged us down. The sun shone brightly through a clear sky and bounced onto my face from every direction. Despite temperatures in the neighborhood of –5° C to –10° C, the bright reflection was tanning my face.

Sled dogs are happy only when they are pulling. They hate to stop. This desire for forward motion never ceases. Our dogs barked loudly throughout our lunch breaks, sometimes leaping into the air trying to pull the anchored sled forward. On trail, they pull with all their might; when thirsty, they scoop snow up into their mouths without breaking stride. "Doggin' it" is a grossly inappropriate expression for lazy behaviour.

Day 4

I wandered off the packed trail at lunch break today with the hope of taking a photo of my dog team, but was forced to turn around when I sank up to my waist in the snow. Our last night was spent at Three Mile Lake Camp, which we shared with a group from France. The French spoke a few words of English, but no German. The Germans in our group spoke broken English, but no French. Aside from one of the guides, who was bilingual, we Canadians knew a few phrases in French, but no German. To say that inter-group communication was interesting would be an understatement. At first, we were kept busy with camp duties; cultural gaps were crossed with smiles and nods. But dinner loosened up the vocal cords. By the time our guides broke out dessert, everyone was trying to *parle francais* or *sprechen die deutsche* between bites of chocolate brownies and strawberry cheesecake. As the clock ticked toward 9:00 p.m. on the last night of our adventure, a healthy fatigue spread through the groups. We planned tomorrow's route back to the Expedition Headquarters before turning in for the night. It wasn't long before we were "snoring the same language".

8.2

Wayne Van Sickle

CANOE TRIP
JOURNAL

Canoe tripping in Algonquin is like no other experience on the planet. When word got out that my good friend Mark and I were planning a 10-day trip during the peak of the autumn colours, there wasn't a person we knew who wasn't jealous. A mutual friend named Todd called to invite himself and his musician friend Tyler along.

Selected memories from our adventure:

Day 1
We unloaded our canoes in the late morning under slightly overcast skies at Canoe Lake. After paying for our permits, we pushed off from shore. As we paddled forward, a slight wind bore down on us from the north. It did little to stop us and was easily overpowered by our excitement at being underway. Crossing an Algonquin lake by canoe is a timeless experience. Gazing out across the lake and thinking about the journey ahead, I felt like one of the many fur traders who paddled these same waters in the mid-to-late 1800's. We travelled up the middle of the lake, propelled only by the power in our bodies and the teamwork among us. Later that afternoon, as we reached the northern extremity of the lake, we heard a noise not unlike the "mooing" of a domestic cow. Peering into the trees, we spied a large female moose sitting on the ground, perhaps 20 metres away. It was mating season for Park moose and this female's call was communicating her level of receptiveness to any love-struck Bull Moose that might be in the area. We floated offshore for several minutes and moved on after everyone had a good close up view of her through the binoculars.

Around the next bend we spied a landing marked by a bright yellow sign indicating the footpath ("portage") to Joe Lake, which lay roughly 300 metres away. We pulled the boats up onto the shore and unloaded our gear. Grasping the canoe along the near gunwales, I tilted it up on its side, lifted it to my knees, reached out for the middle thwart with both hands and swung it upside down and onto my shoulders. I marched off down the trail with the added weight of a small pack on my back. Todd did the same with the other canoe, while Mark and Tyler carried the remaining packs. The weight of ten days of food and gear made us wish we had left a few more items at home!

Ten minutes later we arrived at Joe Lake. After putting our boats in the water, we paused for a drink and a couple of handfuls of peanuts and raisins. The sky had cleared and the wind had ceased to be a factor. We pressed onward. It was close to 5 p.m. when we arrived at Burnt Island Lake where we had reserved one of its many individual campsites. Famished from a hard day of paddling and portaging, we pulled our canoes up at the first available site and scrambled up the short but steep incline to survey our home for the night. It consisted of a small clearing along the rocky but treed shoreline and came complete with a ring of stones signifying the firepit, a few flat places where campers before us had pitched their tents and a wooden box-like privy. Todd and I set up a tent for each of the two canoe teams, while Mark unpacked the cook stove and went about preparing dinner. Tyler got busy filtering drinking water from the lake and scrounging up deadfall for the evening campfire.

The smell of pesto soon permeated the air and lured us to the cook, who, fortunately, had prepared enough for seconds. We had our fill. With a full stomach, and a tent pitched behind me, I was as happy as a canoe tripper could be. I sat on the rocks overlooking the now still lake and watched the sun slip past the horizon in a silent golden blaze. I felt privileged to be in the company of friends amid such beauty.

Day 2

The lake lapped rhythmically onto the shore throughout the night and helped contribute to a long peaceful sleep. Not one of us stirred before 9 a.m. We dismantled our tents and packed up after savouring several bowls of rice porridge topped with dried berries and shaved almonds. The morning sky was clear. The far side of the lake beckoned. We pushed off from shore and paddled out into the great open expanse that was Burnt Island Lake. Thickly forested hills, painted with the deep orange, yellow and red autumn leaves of Maple trees, rose in all directions above a green rim of shoreline Pine trees. Offset by the deep blueness of the lake, it was the unmistakable glory of Ontario in the fall. We checked our map and set a northeasterly course across the big lake toward the 790 m portage to Little Otter Slide Lake.

We had lunch at the far end of the portage on the shores of Little Otterslide Lake. A beaver, towing a branch several times longer than itself, swam by as we munched quietly on sliced cucumbers and rye bread crackers, dipped in chickpea hummus. That night we made camp on an island on Big Trout Lake. Darkness found us sitting around a campfire, trading our favourite stories and reliving the events of the past two days. We turned in relatively early, but were awakened at 3 a.m. by an excited Todd who had discovered the Northern Lights dancing high above the lake in the night sky (you never know what you'll find by wandering out into the Algonquin night in search of the toilet!). One moment the ghostly patterns of green and white hung like giant curtains blowing in a soft wind, the next they seemed to pulsate with the beating of my heart, flashing up into the night sky like spotlights reaching for a common point high overhead.

Day 4

The late afternoon skies, which had been clouding over all day, were rapidly filling with power as we paddled into the narrows of Cat Fish Lake. There were no two ways about it – a storm was approaching. We hurried to get camp set up before the rain arrived. We selected another island campsite. It rose steeply from the waters and provided a commanding view over the expanse of the lake. We pitched the tents in the highest, most protected places and hung a large tarp between several trees. We gathered under it just as the rain started falling. When darkness came, it brought with it thunder and lightning of such intensity that it made us cringe and survey our immediate surroundings. The rain, which had been nothing short of torrential, eventually tapered off to drizzle. The wind died, but the great electrical storm continued to rage. From under our tarp, we looked out across the lake and watched the lightning strike repeatedly behind the rolling hills in the distance. The boom of the thunder followed faint glows appearing over the faraway hills. It made us think of a war-torn place being relentlessly shelled. The power of the electrical storm was unmatched by any I had ever witnessed. We ventured out from under our tarp and sat amid the rocks at the edge of our high castle-like island in pursuit of a more panoramic view of the strikes, but great forks of lightning shot across the sky above us and drove us back to our tarp.

Day 5

The morning air hung heavy over the lake, like the sulphurous cloud left on the ground after a great amount of fireworks is set off. The sky was overcast and grey but the rains had moved on. Today was our scheduled rest day, no long paddles, and no sweaty portages. Cat Fish Lake awaited exploration. Mark and Todd paddled across to the great forests of the mainland to indulge their mutual interest in botany. Tyler headed out in the opposite direction in the other canoe. I stayed back on the island to catch up with my diary, do some quiet reading and take the occasional dip in the cool lake waters. All three explorers returned late in the afternoon and joined me for a leisurely trek around our island.

Day 6
The map told us that this would be our toughest day; circumstances made it our most thrilling. Three portages, including one just shy of 2 km, lay in wait for us. We hurried through the packing up process and pushed off from shore earlier than usual, knowing it would be a long day. It was mid-afternoon by the time we arrived at Manta Lake, a small body of water hardly worth the title. Within minutes we had crossed it and were standing at the start of the day's last but longest portage. With our shoulders still smarting from the previous two portages, we pulled our boats up onto the beach, breathed deeply and prepared ourselves mentally for the long slog through the forest to Hogan Lake. We took several breaks and traded off frequently between carrying the canoe and carrying the packs. After thirty-seven sweaty, backbreaking minutes, I finally reached the end. I threw down the heavy packs I had carried, tore off my clothes and plunged into the refreshing waters of the lake. I heard splash after splash behind me as my weary mates followed my lead.

We were still swimming in Hogan Lake when a loud grunt behind us informed us that we weren't alone. We turned to see a massive 500 kg Bull Moose standing just metres away at the water's edge! His huge rack of antlers, the size of a piano bench, swayed as he turned his large snout back and forth taking in the scents of four startled naked men. We stood perfectly still in the shallow waters. Our eyes were as big as saucers; our hearts stopped beating. We hardly had a moment to react before the great creature snorted indignantly and walked swiftly off into the woods. With adrenaline still coursing through our veins, we remained absolutely still, listening to the snapping branches and sloshing puddles of his departure. Sheepishly, we walked in to shore and put our clothes back on.

We paddled north toward the next adventure of our ten-day odyssey.

The locations of our nightly campsites:
Burnt Island Lake - Big Trout Lake - Burntroot Lake - Catfish Lake (2 nights) - Hogan Lake - Big Trout Lake - Burnt Island Lake (2 nights).

=8.3=

Wayne Van Sickle

BACKPACKING TRIP JOURNAL

For as far back as I can remember, my family has rented a cottage in Northern Ontario each summer. Although my younger sister Diane and I spent many childhood days together exploring nearby forests and lakeshores, we never had the chance to go camping together. Diane also regretted that she had never been a part of a true backcountry experience. We decided to rectify these conditions by planning a short backpacking trip into the Algonquin Park Interior – just the two of us.

Algonquin's multi-loop trail system provides a wide variety of experiences, ranging from epic hikes longer than a week, to shorter adventures like our weekend getaway. We planned to hike roughly four kilometres into the Interior, by way of the Western Uplands Backpacking Trail and set up a two-night camp. We would take short day hikes, and enjoy long conversations. We hoped for clear evenings that would enable stargazing and warm campfires.

We pulled into the parking lot at the trailhead shortly before noon on a clear day in late May. It was perfect hiking weather, sufficiently cool for long pants, but sunny enough to keep our faces warm and our spirits high. We removed our watches, helped each other on with our big packs and crossed the bridge over the Oxtongue River. Marching off into the Algonquin Interior, we turned our backs on our increasingly busy lifestyles. The trail, still partly muddy in sections, led us into a bright green forest where buds on the Maples and other deciduous trees were just opening up. I felt the worries of the "real world" slipping further away with each step. A songbird chirped just above my head. Below, I heard the various peeps and shuffles of the forest floor's inhabitants.

Algonquin's interior trails rarely stay flat for long and we soon came upon our first incline. Putting one foot in front of the other, we ascended the path worn into the hill by those who went before us. The rise and fall of Algonquin's trails rarely amount to anything a reasonably fit person can't handle, but their sheer number requires even the fittest hiker to pause frequently to catch his breath.

After a brief rest we hiked onward. Lush spring greenery and brightly coloured wildflowers, such as the Red Trillium and Yellow Trout-lily, held us in constant awe. We paused frequently to take in the scent of a flower or to investigate an animal noise. At length, the trail descended to the shores of Guskewau Lake – our home for the weekend. Taking off our packs, we trekked about the small blue lake and compared its available campsites. All Interior sites are located on the shores of a lake or the banks of a river and come complete with a fire pit and a wooden toilet privy, set on top of a pit. We selected a site that was large, flat, well-treed and far enough from the main trail that we wouldn't hear other hikers travelling by. Its western exposure would provide us with evening sun, while protecting us from the morning rays that might otherwise threaten to wake us prematurely from the lengthy sleep-ins we looked forward to. After pitching our lightweight tent, we split up the remaining duties. Diane organized our sleeping bags, mattresses and clothes inside the tent, while I hung a tarp among the nearby trees. Firewood was collected and stashed under the tarp for the evening's campfire. After unpacking the kitchen equipment, we finally slowed down to enjoy our site. Diane curled up in the sun with a good book; I set off into the bushes to explore our immediate surroundings. It wasn't too long before hunger led me back to camp, where Diane was already busy adding juice crystals to water filtered from the lake. I fired up the cook stove, and in no time was garnishing a pot of warm pasta with a tomato sauce, fresh spices and vegetables. Thickly sliced rye bread toasted over the camp-stove and romano cheese packed in a zip lock bag rounded out the meal nicely.

We settled in around a warm campfire just as darkness fell on the lake. Ever since the day when mankind first discovered fire, the flicker of the flame has had both a hypnotic, as well as a social effect on humans. Diane and I revived the lost art of conversation and recounted many of our childhood memories.

As the evening progressed, talking increasingly gave way to yawning and we decided to turn in. In no time whatsoever, we were drifting off to sleep, headed toward the long peaceful sleeps that I had assured my sister would accompany our trip. No clocks, no traffic, no neighbours - we were destined to sleep 'til noon. And sleep we did. At least until rudely awakened at dawn by loud sloshing and sucking noises coming from directly behind our tent. Annoyed and groggy, I poked my head out of the tent in a bid to silence whatever it was that was making the noises. My annoyance immediately gave way to wonder as my eyes came to rest on the source. With no time to explain, I dragged my tired, complaining, sleep-deprived sister the length of the tent, shook the sleep out of her eyes, and presented her with the view that every camper wants to see. A mother moose stood in the shallow water just metres offshore with her newborn calf. The pair gazed at us for a moment and then sloshed out of sight. After their departure, we giggled with excitement and promptly fell back to sleep.

I awoke again a few hours later. Taking great pains not to wake my still-snoozing sister, I slipped quietly out of the tent, and tiptoed to the water's edge for my ritual morning swim. Tragically, I had forgotten that it was early spring and not midsummer. Diane was jarred roughly from her sleep by a high-pitched scream as I surfaced amid the frigid waters! After a warm breakfast of instant oatmeal and tea, we packed ourselves a lunch and left camp to spend the day hiking along the main trail. Without the heavy packs that weighed us down the day before, we felt as if we were flying. We spotted a beaver lodge and watched two loons fish the shores of a nearby lake before returning to camp for dinner.

The stars were brilliant that night, and before turning in, we sprawled out on the rocks along the lakeshore and gazed up at them. We identified as many constellations as we could and philosophized about our place in this vast universe. We then quickly fell asleep, once again anticipating a lengthy sleep-in. The forest's inhabitants had other plans for us. Once again, we were awakened abruptly at dawn. Eerie sounds filled the morning air and caused our pulses to quicken and the hair to stand up on the backs of our necks. We sat bolt upright in our sleeping bags amid the howls of a pack of wolves. The howls were so clear and loud, that it sounded as if the pack was standing on the shores of our lake! After shaking off the initial alarm that such a noise causes, we lay back down in our sleeping bags and listened to the wild chorus of voices. The unforgettable choir went on for several moments. We could pick out individual howls but it was difficult to make a guess as to how many wolves we were hearing. We applauded as the last note faded. Then we promptly fell back to sleep.

Once again I awoke before Diane. I slipped quietly out and prepared myself as I walked to the water's edge. I bit down hard on my lip and dove into the refreshing waters of this magical place. Later, as we hiked back to the car, I wished that we could have stayed another day. Who knows what event might have accompanied the sunrise?

9.1

Chris Boettger

LOON
(Gavia immer)

Weight:	Approx 4 kg
Bill to tail length:	70 - 90 cm
Wingspan:	Approx 150 cm
Diet:	Fish
Chance of seeing:	High from May to Nov, Not in Park Dec to Apr

About the Loon

The loon holds a special place in the hearts of Canadians, who have come to regard it as a symbol of our wilderness. Its portrait graces the back of the twenty-dollar bill, as well as the back of the one-dollar coin, which we affectionately refer to as the "loonie. Paintings of the loon and its black and white checked coat hang in many Canadian homes and government buildings. The distinctive calls of the loon echo through the night air in natural places such as Algonquin Park, and seem to call us away from our fast-paced lives, beckoning us back to nature. These calls have such a special quality that they never fail to work magic on our souls. In fact, I've never known anyone to grow tired of them - not even those lucky enough to live on a northern lake. Loons nest on the majority of Algonquin's lakes and seem to call out nightly. The chances of hearing their calls are extremely good if you are in the Park overnight in the summer.

Seasonal Migration

Loons live in Algonquin Park from late April to November. Before the Park's lakes freeze over in the winter, they fly thousands of kilometres to the southern USA, where they live in the warm Atlantic waters off the coast of Florida. There they fish and bide their time until April, when they fly back to Algonquin Park's newly thawed lakes. Loons can fly at speeds of up to 120 km/h. They posses a special gland that excretes salt from their system and enables them to live in both the salt waters of the ocean, and the fresh waters of Ontario's lakes. They shed their striking black and white checked coat when they fly south, and grow a drab, plainly coloured grey coat in its place. They also refrain from making their amazing calls until they return to the north-country.

What Loons Eat

The bulk of the loon's diet is small to medium sized fish, with perch being highly preferred. The average adult loon eats up to a kilogram of fish each day! They spy these fish with their keen eyes and dive under the water, catching them in their bills. The large webbed feet positioned toward the rear of their bodies enable them to swim quickly enough to overtake the fastest of fish. Loons have the amazing ability to hold their breath for long periods of time under water. I have seen loons remain under the surface for over three minutes, surfacing over 50 m away from the place where they dove.

The loon graces the back of Canada's one dollar coin

These amazing capabilities also enable them to escape from threatening situations.

A Loon's Enemies

The young loon faces threats from above and below the water, as well as from predators living on dry land. Raccoons love the taste of loon eggs, and chase parents off the nest in order to feast on their eggs. After hatching, the young may be taken by hawks, which swoop down from the skies, or by large snapping turtles and fish that live in the lakes. Adult loons, however, are quite safe from harm in Algonquin Park. It is rare for one to die here. Most loon deaths occur in the winter months when they are waiting out the Canadian freeze in the warm coastal waters off Florida. Many are taken by ocean predators such as sharks, or perish from disease caused by the high levels of pollution and oil slicks found in the American waters.

Family Life

Loons mate for life. They spend winters apart, but return to

Chris Boettger

Loons nest very close to the water's edge

Algonquin each summer to mate and share the responsibilities of raising their offspring. Loons prefer to use the same lake every year, and often have it all to themselves unless it is big enough to provide adequate food and privacy for another pair. Shortly after returning to their lake in April, the loon couple builds a nest made from vegetation and mud on the shore, in an area with clear, shallow water and protection from the wind. Loons have extreme difficulty walking on land and build their nest less than 100 cm from the water's edge (one of the reasons why loons are vulnerable to fluctuations in water levels). This difficulty on land is the result of the positioning of their feet and is the trait that earned them their name. "Loon" is a derivation of a Scandinavian word meaning "lame".

Loons engage in subtle courtship rituals of synchronous diving and head rubbing before mating, which is quickly accomplished on land in under ten seconds! The female loon lays two olive green-brown eggs and shares the responsibility of sitting on the eggs for one month with her mate. In late June, the eggs hatch and the young loons are able to swim one half day later. For the first week of their life they are unable to catch their own food and are fed small fish by their parents. Later, they are taught to hunt by dropping injured fish in front of them. The chicks often ride on their parent's backs to protect themselves against fatigue, cold waters and predators. By the 11th week of life, the young loons are able to care for themselves and fly long distances. Some of them leave the lake to find other young loons with whom they will make the long flight south for the winter. Loons have their own young when they are four years old.

Loon Calls

Although loon calls are not totally understood, they appear to fall into four major categories, each facilitating communication among loons or conveying information regarding their emotional states.

- *Tremelo* – sounds somewhat like laughter, but appears to signify alarm or distress. It can be given in response to an approaching boat or a disturbance to the nest. It is also the only call given in flight.
- *Wail* – sometimes likened to the sound a lone wolf howl. It is given when an individual loon is separated from its partner or chicks. It appears to indicate a desire to interact with or rejoin that family member.
- *Yodel* – spectacular undulating calls uttered exclusively by males. These are given during territorial confrontations with other loons.
- *Hoot* – quick and short one "syllable" calls that maintain contact between individual loons in a family group or late summer flock.

Where and How to See a Loon

Loons are relatively easy to encounter in Algonquin Park as a majority of lakes are home to a pair each summer. They often remain in the waters of their lake throughout the entire day and therefore can be seen at any time of the day. Visitors might see loons in any of the lakes along the highway. A few places that I have found to be

particularly reliable for loon spotting are:
1) Found Lake (km 20). Park in the parking lot and walk to the shore, less than 15 metres away.
2) Lake of Two Rivers (km 33). Check the shoreline along the highway.
3) Brewer Lake (km 48.6)
4) Costello Lake (km 46.3). Also check the mouth of the creek at the end of Opeongo Road.

The Algonquin Park Loon Survey
In 1983, Park officials decided to track the reproductive success of Algonquin's loons. The survey relies heavily on the sightings of Park Visitors. Visitors contribute by documenting their sightings in a binder located in the Visitor Centre reception area and recording whether or not they observed chicks with the adult(s). Park naturalists analyze the body of sightings at the end of the season. First they determine the total number of lakes upon which loons were reported, and then they calculate the percentage of those lakes where reproduction occurred. Reproduction on any given lake is established by multiple sightings of chicks. Results are published yearly in the Visitors' Newsletter. In the past, the rate of successful reproduction has varied from a low of 21% to a high of 50%. Although this distribution is seemingly large, it tends to cluster around 40%, and Park naturalists feel that there is neither a long-term increase nor a decrease trend at work.

Precautions
- Do not approach or disturb loons on their nest. If harassed, hatching may be unsuccessful.

Further Interest:
- Loon sightings are recorded in a book at the Visitor Centre. If you haven't had luck finding one, take a gander at the latest sightings. Park staff can direct you to these lakes although many may not be accessible by road.
- Mounted loons are on display at the Visitor Centre.
- A cassette tape entitled *Voices of Algonquin**, contains amazing recordings of loon calls. Narration by Ron Tozer explains the meanings of the different calls. Several other recordings put to music are also available at the Visitor Centre.

9.2

Chris Boettger

MOOSE
(Alces alces)

Weight:	300 - 500 kg
Shoulder height:	150 – 200 cm
Head and body length:	250 – 300 cm
Diet:	Vegetarian
Chance of seeing:	Excellent in May & Jun, Good from Jul to Nov, Moderate from Nov to Apr

About the Moose

The moose is the largest animal found in Algonquin Park. A fully grown Algonquin male, which is only slightly bigger than the female, may weigh close to 500 kg!!! If you have the opportunity to observe a moose, you might conclude from its long, skinny legs and its slow movements that it is a clumsy creature. Nothing is farther from the truth. A moose can outrun most domestic dogs, and travel through the thickest forest with grace. Like many of the animals living in the Park, the moose has poor eyesight, which is compensated for by senses of smell and hearing that far exceed our own. Moose live in many parts of Canada, both to the east and to the west of the Park. Algonquin has one of the highest concentrations of moose in the entire world. Park naturalists estimate that there are between 2,000 and 3,000 moose in Algonquin. We Canadians have a certain fondness for the creature. The moose appears regularly in the names of our restaurants and pubs. There is even a popular brand of beer called "Moosehead" which features a bull moose with an impressive set of antlers on the label. Communities such as Moose Jaw, Saskatchewan have gone as far as to name themselves after the great animal. Here in Ontario, Moose Factory, Moose River and Moosonee are all located within 100 km of each other.

What a Moose Eats

Moose are total vegetarians. They wander the Park eating different plants, depending on the time of the year. In the winter, when little else is available, the moose's diet is comprised almost entirely of twigs and tree branches. It may eat up to 20 kg of tree branches in one day! In fact, the name "moose" comes from an old Native American word meaning "twig eater". After a long winter of eating trees, moose crave salt and therefore select food high in sodium for the rest of the year. One way Algonquin's moose find salt is by drinking from the pools of water that form by the side of Highway 60 from late April until mid-June. These pools are high in sodium because truckloads of salt are dumped on the road throughout the winter to prevent dangerous ice buildup. This is why it is so easy to see a moose in the spring by simply driving up the highway. Aquatic plants that are rich in sodium begin to grow in mid-June and form the bulk of the moose's diet until they disappear in the fall, leaving the great creatures with little else but those tasty twigs.

A close-up enounter with a moose.

A Moose's Enemies

Black bears and wolves prey upon young moose, but a healthy, full-grown moose in Algonquin Park has few predators. Algonquin's moose may live as long as 20 years. Occasionally a pack of wolves may attack, but a healthy moose can usually defend itself, crippling the would-be predator with a single kick from its powerful long legs, or inflicting deep cuts with its sharp hooves. A much more serious threat comes in the form of a bloodsucking winter tick (*Dermacentor albipictus*), whose activity causes itching moose to scratch off patches of their own hair. Extreme infestation can cause significant hair loss, and is a factor in some winter deaths.

Family Life

Moose do not build dwellings. They are truly the free spirits of Algonquin, wandering about, simply lying down to sleep when tired. Adult males and females do not roam together or form lasting bonds. They lead rather solitary lives coming together only once a year in late September or early October to mate. Afterwards, the animals part to resume their wanderings. Females give birth to one or two young in late May, often swimming out to islands to seek haven from predators. Calves weigh between 10 and 15 kg and learn to walk within a few days. The young moose travel with their mother for a year before striking out on their own. Female moose are fit to bear young by their third year, while males generally don't earn the right to mate until they are five or six years old. The ease with which a male finds a mate is determined by the size of its antlers.

Antlers and Mating

Antlers are carried exclusively by males. They grow a new set of antlers or "racks" each April. These fall off sometime between December and February. The healthier the moose, the larger its antlers. A moose in the prime of his life (four to eight years old) grows a hard, "boney", set weighing up to 25 kg and spanning over a metre from tip to tip. Younger and older males grow smaller racks. The purpose of these racks is to ensure that the strongest and healthiest males sire the offspring. In September, males search for a mate and respond to the calls of receptive female moose. Should two males meet in front of the same female, only the stronger male with the larger set of antlers gets to mate. In such an encounter, the smaller male usually concedes to the bigger moose and leaves the area. However, if both males are roughly the same size, and have equally large antlers, they may fight to determine who is the stronger. The two males, each weighing up to 500 kg, put their heads down, lock antlers and push against each other. This continues until one of the animals concedes victory and leaves. The victor then mates with the female.

How and Where to See a Moose

Consult the animal viewing section of the *Activities* chapter for the best options by car, foot or canoe. Driving "the circuit" during prime wildlife hours is the best tactic for moose viewing at any time of the year. Visitors are virtually guaranteed of seeing moose by the roadside from late-April to early June; I have heard of people seeing up to 15 moose in one circuit. In the summer, moose will be spotted standing in lakes, ponds and rivers. This is the most fruitful time of the year for moose encounters along the hiking trails. Along the highway, they are most frequently spotted between km 25 and the East Gate. Moose are seen with less frequency in the fall and winter, but can still be spotted crossing the highway or nibbling at roadside trees.

Precautions

1) Moose frequently run out in front of cars or simply just stand in the middle of the highway. They can be extremely difficult to see at night. Each year over 30 Park moose are killed in automobile collisions. Moose/car collisions cause major damage to vehicles and have resulted in the loss of human life. I once had the misfortune to hit a moose - it was one of the saddest and most terrifying experiences

Wayne Van Sickle

More than 30 moose/automobile collisions occur annually in Algonquin Park.

of my life. Risk can be reduced by driving below the 80 km/h speed limit and by keeping an eye out for moose. Their eyes, which reflect the light from headlights, can often be seen from a distance.

2) Moose can commonly be viewed safely from outside your car. However, they are wild animals with the ability to hurt us severely; stay back at least 20 metres and do not pursue them when they wander off.

Further Interest:
- Recordings of various moose calls can be found on *Voices of Algonquin Park** a cassette narrated by Ron Tozer who explains what is being heard.
- Mounted moose are on permanent display at the Visitor Centre.

9.3

Algonquin Park Museum

BEAVER
(Castor canadensis)

Weight:	18 - 36 kg
Head and body length:	65 – 75 cm
Tail:	23 – 30 cm long,
	11 – 15 cm wide
Diet:	Herbivore
Chance of seeing:	High from Apr through Oct
	Slim from Nov through Mar

About the Beaver

The beaver is one of the world's most unique animals. It has many special physical characteristics including see-through eyelids and bright orange teeth which never stop growing. No other creature found on the planet, aside from man, changes the physical environment more to meet its own needs. The beaver can turn small streams into ponds or even lakes by holding back the water with dams constructed out of sticks and mud. Beavers change their immediate environment to the point that several plant and animal species, previously unable to live in the area, are able to thrive after the arrival of a beaver colony. Beavers are found throughout Canada and are regarded as one of the primary symbols of our country. They are pictured on the back of the five-cent coin. Beavers are no slackers. In fact, they can cut down as many as 200 trees each year! This work ethic is one of the reasons that we hold them up as role models to our children. The scouting movement's introductory program for girls and boys aged five to seven is called "Beavers". It promotes a love of the outdoors, hard work and helping family.

Amazing Physical Characteristics

Beavers spend most of their time in the water and are uniquely adapted to their water-based life. Special muscles seal off ears and nostrils to prevent water from leaking in when they dive. They also have see-through eyelids that enable underwater vision and the ability to hold their breath for up to ten minutes. Perhaps the most amazing part of a beaver is its mouth. Beavers have lips that close behind their teeth so they can chew on plants and trees under water without swallowing a belly full of water! Beavers have bright orange teeth that never stop growing. They require periodic trimming, which is accomplished by chewing on tree parts. Large flat tails act like rudders, steering the creatures as they tow heavy branches across the water for use in building their homes or dams. Beavers have two layers of fur to keep them dry and warm. They also secrete a natural oil from a gland near their tail that keeps their fur waterproof. Beavers can see almost as well as a human during the day, but they have poor night vision. They compensate for this poor night vision with an extremely keen sense of hearing.

What Beavers Eat

A beaver's favourite meal is tree bark. It chews it off trees and grinds it up with its sharp teeth. Beavers leave the water to search

One of the many beaver lodges visible from Highway 60.

for their favourite bark. They also eat tree buds, shrubs and water plants. Because they are more vulnerable to predators on land than in the water, they often take their meal back to their home in the water to eat it in safety. Beginning in October, beavers eat as much tree bark as they possibly can in order to fatten themselves up for the long winter.

A Beaver's Enemies
Algonquin Park's beavers are preyed upon primarily by wolves. Although beavers are safe inside their lodges and are rarely caught when in water, they are an easy catch when encountered on land. Large webbed feet, which enable them to swim so well, make them as clumsy and relatively slow on land as you or I would be in scuba flippers. Beavers slap their tail on top of the water to alert one another to the presence of danger.

A Beaver's Home
Beavers' homes are called lodges. They build their lodges in ponds or lakes, out of tree branches and mud. Beavers cut down trees, float the branches across the water, and deposit them in a pile that begins on the bottom of the pond and grows to about one metre

Beaver dams are frequent obstacles for multi-day canoe trippers.

above water. The beaver then packs mud on the outside of the pile to strengthen it. When this is done, it dives under the water and chews a tunnel through the sticks into the centre of the pile. Once there, it chews out a small room a few centimetres above the water level. This room gets air from the outside through small holes in the roof of the mud-packed structure. The only entrance or exit to this room is through the underwater tunnel. You can see beaver lodges in many of the small lakes and ponds along the highway, including Eucalia Lake at km 39, or by hiking the Beaver Pond Trail, which takes hikers within view of several lodges. There is also a beaver lodge on display at the Visitor Centre, complete with mounted beavers.

Beginning in the fall, beavers collect and store food for the coming winter. They pile branches and tree parts at the bottom of their lake or pond. Beavers spend the winter inside their lodges but exit it periodically by way of the underwater tunnel to retrieve food from the pile. Shallow bodies of water freeze solid in the cold Algonquin winter. If the waters of the beaver colony's pond were to freeze from top to bottom, the beavers would no longer be able to reach its food stores. To ensure winter survival, beavers raise water levels in their pond by building dams wherever water naturally exits their pond. Like their lodges, these dams are built with trees that they cut down. They ram sticks and branches into the muddy river bottom and pile additional sticks on top of them. They strengthen the

Beavers are most active in the evenings. They are most easily spotted in calm water by looking for the "V" shaped wake they produce when swimming.

structure with a thick layer of mud. Scientists have demonstrated, with the use of recordings of running water, that the beaver's building behaviour is instinctually activated by the sound of running water.

Family Life
Adult beavers mate for life. They share the responsibilities of raising their offspring and building and repairing their dams. Mating takes place during the cold Algonquin winter in late January or early February and four kits are born three and a half months later. The young are born with sharp teeth and are able to swim within a few hours of birth. The mother keeps them in the lodge for about two months to nurse them. In summer, the young beavers emerge from the lodge. They live with their parents for two years before they strike out on their own to create their own families.

How and Where to See Beavers
Beavers are extremely common in Algonquin Park. In fact, the Park supports about one beaver colony for each square kilometre. Despite this fact, they can be difficult to spot because they spend most of their time in the water and swim with only their noses and ears above water. However, you have a reasonably good chance if you

heed the following tips:

1) October is the best month for spotting beavers - they are very active repairing their dams and can be seen throughout the day. Those wishing to look for them from April through September should concentrate their efforts around sunset.

2) Beavers are most easily spotted when the lake is smooth and wave-free. You can find them by looking for the V-shaped wake they create when swimming.

3) Concentrate your efforts on **small** lakes and ponds. I have had good luck along Highway 60 at Eucalia Lake at km 39 as well as at Costello Lake at Opeongo Road (km 45) where I have seen beavers swim right through the culvert which links water on both sides of the highway.

4) The Beaver Pond Trail at km 45.2, which was specifically designed to view the work of beavers, and the low-lying wet area along the Mizzy Lake Trail at km15.4 are also great places.

5) You can always count on a close-up sighting at the Visitor Centre, where mounted beavers are on permanent display.

9.4

Andrew Mills

RACCOON
(Procyon lotor)

Weight:	7 - 9 kg
Head and body length:	40 - 70 cm
Tail:	20 – 40 cm
Diet:	Omnivore
Chance of seeing:	High at night, Low during the day

About the Raccon
Raccoons are among the more intelligent animals in Algonquin Park. They thrive in the lake and stream environment, which provides great hunting grounds. They have also learned to take full advantage of Park visitors and raid campgrounds nightly, making off with food. Their adorable faces seem to lead many campers to tolerate their troublesome antics. However, they can be a real nuisance. I have been awakened in my tent on more than one occasion by raccoons knocking over pots and rooting through my gear, searching for food. They have paws similar to human hands, and are able to open jars and unhook coolers and other containers. Raccoons always seem to find that special treat mistakenly left by the fireside at bedtime. I have lost more than one bag of potato chips this way!!!

Physical Attributes and Abilities
A raccoon is a little bigger than a large house cat. Its most defining features are the colouring on its face, which makes it appear to be wearing a black mask, and its long bushy tail, which has a black tip and five to seven black rings along its length. They use these big tails for balance when climbing out onto branches, and also as warm blankets to curl up with in the winter. Raccoons have two layers of fur: a thick inner coat that keeps them warm, and an outer coat made of long, smooth fur, that keeps them dry. Raccoons tend to sleep during the day and are most active at night. They have extremely good night vision, and like many animals in the Park, have sharp senses of smell and hearing. Raccoons are master climbers and scurry up the nearest tree when threatened. They are also good swimmers, and can run as fast as 25 km/h over short distances.

What a Raccoon Eats
Raccoons have one of the most diverse diets of any animal in the Park. Most commonly, they eat food found at the water's edge, such as frogs, clams, crayfish and minnows; however, they will also eat mice, turtles, snakes, and birds eggs. They are the loon's most feared enemy, and will steal their eggs by chasing the parental loon off the nest. In the summertime, raccoons enjoy berries, nuts, seeds, grasshoppers, beetles and crickets. Highway 60 raccoons also dine on a wide range of donuts, potato chips, pickles, cheeses and other store-bought goods liberated from campers. Raccoons usually establish a feeding territory, between two and three square kilometres in size, in which they are the only raccoon. However, they have been known to share food-rich areas, such as campgrounds, with other raccoons.

Some authorities are of the opinion that raccoons are more intelligent than cats.

A Raccoon's Enemies

Larger owls prey upon young raccoons, but adult raccoons have few predators due to their size, speed and ability to climb trees when in danger. Wolves and fishers (*Martes pennanti*) occasionally capture raccoons.

A Raccon's Home

Raccoons build their dens in caves, trees, hollow stumps or logs, which they line with wood chips and leaves. Raccoons sleep in their homes for the majority of the day, and awaken at night to search for food. They spend the majority of the cold Algonquin winter in their homes sleeping, but unlike the chipmunk, they do not stockpile food for the winter. Instead, they eat extra food in the fall in order to build up a thick layer of fat from which they can draw nutrients while they sleep. They also venture out into the snowy forests to look for food on warm sunny days.

Family Life

Raccoons live by themselves except in the late spring when they mate. During this time, males search the forest for a female. If two males meet in front of the same female, they fight to earn the right to mate with her, although the female may not always be receptive to the victor. Raccoon couples share a den for a two-week period during which time they mate repeatedly. Afterwards they split up, and the female is left on her own to raise the four or five cubs that are born approximately nine weeks later. Born helpless and unable to open their eyes for three weeks, the young remain in the den for two months and are fed by their mother who leaves nightly to find food. Afterwards, the mother brings them outside to learn foraging and hunting skills. The young raccoons spend the winter with their mother in her den and are ready to live independently by the following spring.

Where and How to See Raccoons

Raccoons are seen during the night. You will rarely see them during the day as they are usually sleeping in the dens. They are frequently encountered in Park campgrounds after dark in the summer or fall, going through some unlucky camper's cooler or garbage. They make their appearance after the majority of campers have retired for the evening. Look for their eyes which brightly reflect light.

Precautions

1) Campers should ensure that all food and garbage is placed in their vehicle, and that all pots are cleaned by nightfall. Those without a vehicle should place all food and garbage in a bag and suspend it with rope from a large tree branch. The bag should hang at least 4 m (13 feet) off the ground, and 2 m (6 ½ feet) away from the tree trunk.

2) Shining light in their faces, clapping loudly and yelling as you approach slowly usually scares off raccoons found rooting through your things. They will likely retreat slowly. Put the items of interest away immediately or they will soon return. Although raccoons do not usually attack humans, you should be aware that they are tough characters, possessing sharp claws and teeth. One of my earlier memories of Northern Ontario was of my father throwing in the towel in disgust after encountering a raccoon who had gone into the garbage at our cottage. He ran back inside mere seconds after going out to "teach that damn coon a lesson". As he slammed the screen door shut, I could see the large aggressive animal still spitting and hissing. If you encounter a raccoon that appears unwilling to give up its treasure, you may want to throw in the towel as well. You'll know better next time.

9.5

Wayne Van Sickle

CHIPMUNK
(Tamias striatus)

Head and body length:	13 - 16 cm
Diet:	Vegetarian
Weight:	80 – 110 g
Chance of seeing:	Excellent from Apr to Oct, None from Nov to Apr

About the Chipmunk

Chipmunks are extremely common in the Park. Dashing from fallen log to rock, they scurry about the forest floor in a never ending search for food. They rarely stay still for more than a moment. Most people find their sudden movements comical and never grow tired of watching their antics. Chipmunks often approach Park visitors hoping to secure food. They are among the only Park animals that visitors can safely feed. Whether you are hiking along a trail, sitting in your campground reading a book or having a mid-day snack on a rock, expect chipmunks to find you and pick through your things looking for food. In the past, chipmunks have crawled over my boots and even up my back. Once, while taking a break from hiking the Beaver Pond Trail, I watched a chipmunk climb right into my knapsack! Their small size and friendliness never fail to endear them to children who often call them "chippies" and grow up with fond memories of the chipmunks they fed nuts.

A Chipmunk's Home

Chipmunks live under the ground in soccerball-sized dens, which they line with shredded leaves and dry grass to make them more comfortable for sleeping. Each chipmunk digs several tunnels leading to its den. If you look very hard, you might find the entrances to these tunnels under fallen logs, piles of leaves, or at the base of a tree. Amazingly enough, chipmunks rarely wander further than 50 m from their home in which they dwell all of their lives.

What Chipmunks Eat

Chipmunks love fruits such as blueberries and raspberries, as well as seeds like the pine seed. When these are not available, they will also eat wild grasses, mushrooms, roots, bird eggs, grasshoppers, beetles, caterpillars and other insects. Chipmunks often carry their food to a high place such as a stump or rock before eating, to keep an eye out for danger. Chipmunks can safely be fed peanuts, other nuts or granola placed upon a rock next to you. On occasion, they will even take food from your hand! Be aware that their teeth are sharp and can inflict small, but painful cuts.

A Chipmunk's Enemies

Unfortunately for the chipmunk, many animals in Algonquin Park, including snakes, hawks, racoons, weasels and foxes consider them to be tasty snacks! Chipmunks avoid capture by running quickly

Chipmunks are very bold

across open areas, where they are especially vulnerable to attack by birds. They are also very secretive about the location of their dens in order to avoid predators such as the weasel who are able to enter their dens to catch them. An intelligent and lucky chipmunk may live as long as three years.

Family Life
Male and female chipmunks do not live together. They avoid each other most of the time, and come together only briefly in the spring and again in the summer to mate. Males fight for the right to mate with a particular female. Biting is the main tactic in these battles, and when one chipmunk feels that he has had enough, he leaves the victor to mate with the female. After mating, the animals go their separate ways. One month later, the female gives birth to between four and six blind and hairless offspring in her den. The male, long gone by this point, takes no part whatsoever in the raising of his offspring. The young chipmunks remain with their mother for ten weeks, during which time they are fed, played with and taught to gather food. Afterwards, they strike out on their own to build their own den and live independently.

A Chipmunk's Duties

Up to one metre of snow accumulates on the Algonquin forest floor each winter, making it impossible for chipmunks to find new food. They cope by storing sufficient food in their dens to last the entire winter (five months). This means collecting up to sixty thousand seeds and nuts before the first snowfall!!! This tall order keeps chipmunks incredibly busy from July to October. Special cheek pouches that stretch allow these tiny creatures to fill their cheeks with a pile of seeds and nuts almost twice the size of their heads. The insides of these amazing pouches do not get wet like our cheeks, but rather stay dry to protect their food from getting damp as it is transported from forest to den.

A Winter's Sleep

As winter approaches, chipmunks grow an extra thick and warm layer of fur to protect themselves against the cold. They spend the entire winter dozing in their dens, where they wake periodically to eat food from their stores.

Where and How to See a Chipmunk

If you visit a campground, picnic area or hiking trail between May and October, you are virtually guaranteed of seeing these tiny creatures. In fact, they will most likely find you when you break out the lunch. For a close encounter or a good photo, take a bag of nuts or sunflower seeds along and gently toss the food near the chipmunks when they approach. You are not likely to spot a chipmunk when it is raining or hot and sunny because they take shelter inside their dens at these times.

9.6

Andrew Mills

RED FOX
(Vulpes vulpes)

Weight:	3 - 5 kg
Head and body length:	50 - 85 cm
Tail length:	36 – 46 cm
Shoulder height:	30 cm
Diet:	Carnivore
Chance of seeing:	Moderate

About the Fox

Different kinds of foxes are found in many parts of the world, including Europe, North Africa and Asia. The variety found in Algonquin Park is the Red Fox. A Red Fox usually has a red to yellowish-brown coat, which fades to white on its under-parts. Its feet and the backs of its ears are black. Foxes are portrayed as sneaky, sly troublemakers in children's stories. In reality, foxes are relatively intelligent and certainly possess the capacity for sneakiness. They often appear to display curiousity and have been known to follow Park visitors as they walk the trails.

What a Fox Eats

Foxes prefer mice, chipmunks and hares, but will also eat insects, snails, birds' eggs and even berries if food becomes scarce. They usually hunt for their food, but will also scavenge off the remains of wolf or road kills. Foxes, like wolves, maintain a territory in which they have exclusive hunting rights among their species. They mark this territory by urinating upon trees and will fight to defend their rights if another fox does not respect them.

A Fox's Enemies

Great Horned Owls or Fishers (*Martes pennanti*) may take Algonquin's young foxes, while wolves and black bears may prey upon mature foxes. The slyest Park foxes may live to be 12 years old.

Physical Characteristics

Perhaps the most striking feature of a fox is its bushy tail, which is often over half as long as the rest of the animal. It is used to communicate to other foxes by wagging it in particular ways, and it can also be wrapped around the fox's body on a cold night to keep it warm. Unlike black bears and chipmunks that sleep the winter away, foxes hunt throughout the cold season. Their coats thicken as the winter approaches. Foxes have many keen senses. They have large ears that can hear a mouse moving in grass up to 90 m away and a very sensitive nose, which can detect a mouse hiding under snow! They also have good eyesight, 42 sharp teeth and they can run at speeds of up to 72 km/h.

A Fox's Home

Foxes have two different types of dwellings that they use at different times of the year and for different purposes. A shelter den is a small room made within a pile of rocks or dug into a sandy hill. Shelter dens in sandy hills have a short tunnel leading to a small room large enough for the fox to crawl into. In their territory, foxes may have up to a dozen of these dens, which they use when they want to hide from bad weather or a predator. They also spend the hottest hours of the day in these cool dens. The other type of den, known as a birthing den, is used to give birth, and to raise their young. Birthing dens are larger than shelter dens, they are usually dug into sandy hillsides and have several tunnels leading to and from them for safety. Foxes rarely build their dens from scratch. Instead, they find an old den formerly used by a ground hog or other animal and enlarge it to suit themselves.

Family Life

Foxes are solitary creatures. The male and female come together only once each year in January or February to mate. Afterwards, the male resumes his solitary hunting life while the female raises the young. The female retires to her birthing den to have her young roximately 50 days after mating, and gives birth to three to eight

A Fox pup outside the den.

young in March or April. The young are born helpless and cannot see or hear for approximately ten days. They remain inside the protection of the den for one month and are fed by their mother's milk, later they eat meat which is partially digested and regurgitated by their mother. The mother fox encourages her young to chew on sticks, bones and feathers and to play-fight with each other in order to learn hunting and fighting skills. By the time winter arrives in November, the young foxes have learned all they can from their mother and leave her for independent lives.

How and Where to See a Fox
Algonquin's foxes easily overcome the fear of humans. They have been known to unnerve people by following them as they walk along trails. Although Algonquin's foxes have not been known to inflict injury on people, it is important to remember that they are wild animals and therefore are unpredictable. They should not be fed or encouraged to interact with people. Like many Park animals, they are most active at night, and are best looked for in the evening around sunset, or in the early morning. The best way to spot one is to drive "the circuit" as described in the Activities Chapter. You may see them crossing the road or trotting along the open areas by the roadside. You can also look for the shine of their eyes created when the light from your car's headlights strike them.

9.7

DWAYNE HARTY & KEVIN HOCKLEY
Spruce Bog / Wolf Diorama
Algonquin Park Visitor Centre

WOLF
(Canis ? ? ?)

Weight:	30 kg
Length:	170 cm
Diet:	Carnivore
Chance of seeing:	Rarely seen but often heard

About the Wolf

Wolves are portrayed in children's stories such as the Three Little Pigs, and Little Red Riding Hood, as dangerous, bloodthirsty and evil. Legends about the werewolf, a half man - half wolf creature, insist they attack and kill people. The truth about wolves is that they are highly intelligent creatures living in close-knit family clusters, and that they play with and care for their young. They pose little threat to us. Unfortunately, this reality has been slow to dawn on humans, and we have been the direct cause of significant numbers of wolf deaths. In fact, even Algonquin Park Rangers once hunted wolves in an attempt to rid the Park of them. Luckily they weren't successful and our understanding of the creature has grown. Today, Park naturalists claim that more people hear wolves in the wild right here in Algonquin than in any other place on the face of the Earth!

Algonquin's Wolves

Different types of wolves live in North America. Those found in Algonquin Park have brownish coats with specks of black and white. At around 30 kg, they are among the smallest wolves found on the continent – almost one half the size of the wolves found much farther north in Arctic Canada. Although we know that Algonquin's wolves are special, it is not yet understood just how unique they are. Some recent genetic research suggests that reclassification may be appropriate. They are currently listed as members of a subspecies (*lycaon*) of the Gray Wolf *(Canis lupus)*; however, there is speculation that they may in fact be better classified as Eastern Wolves *(Canis lycaon)* – a unique species of wolf, which would include the endangered Red Wolf of the southern USA. Additional research will undoubtedly shed further light on the matter.

The History of Algonquin Wolves

Although early reports on Algonquin Park indicate that wolves were numerous at the time of the Park's creation in 1893, they were not looked upon with favour. An 1895 report stated that their numbers were too great for the "good of the deer". Evidently it was thought that fewer numbers of wolves would lead to greater numbers of deer. Little effort was made to understand the species, and extermination of wolves became Park policy in the first year of its existence. For thirty years, poison was the principal method of killing them, until it gave way to snaring. The number of wolves killed was mentioned periodically in the reports of the Park Superintendent from 1909 through 1944. The yearly totals were usually somewhere in the neighbourhood of 25 to 55, but reached a high of 128 in 1931. Park-sanctioned killing continued until 1959 when it was discontinued in order to set the stage for an ambitous multi-year study of the dynamics of an uncontrolled wolf population. This study, which made use of aircraft in the winter to track wolves, was the first major attempt to understand wolves and the role they play in the ecosystem. Wolves have been protected within Park boundaries since the time of the study.

What a Wolf Eats

Wolves are meat eaters that hunt both by themselves and in groups. They prey upon animals both larger and smaller than themselves. The bulk of the Algonquin Park wolf diet is comprised of three main prey: white-tailed deer, beavers and moose. Deer are by far the most preferred. This preference is so strong that when the numbers of deer living in Algonquin Park have risen or fallen in the past, the Park's population of wolves has followed suit. Beavers are plentiful in the Park and easy to catch when encountered on land. They are an important seasonal dietary element taken frequently in early spring, late summer and fall. Although wolves do manage to kill both yearling and adult moose, a healthy adult moose tends to stand its ground with remarkable success. Wolves attempting to take down such a moose are in real danger of mortal injuries inflicted by the long powerful legs and sharp hooves. The vast percentage of moose consumed by Algonquin's wolves is by way of scavenging the carcasses of ones that have already died. Such scavenging is most common in late winter.

Wolves possess some amazing abilities that help them catch prey. They can run at a steady pace for several hours at a time and are capable of short bursts of speed of over 45 km/h. They are also great jumpers. Wolves are not always successful hunters and sometimes go days at a time between kills. For this reason, they can eat as much as 15 kg of meat at once.

Predators

Inside Algonquin Park, there is no animal that hunts wolves as a matter of habit. However, the territories of some packs extend beyond the boundaries of Algonquin Park, and numerous wolves are still shot or snared by man when they venture outside of the Park. This is more than unfortunate. Today, we know that wolves pose little danger to man and that they play an important part in Algonquin's complex food web. In fact, many Park animals such as eagles, foxes, martens and ravens benefit greatly from cleaning the bones of wolf kills and scavenging many of the scraps that wolves are not interested in. The average lifespan of an Algonquin wolf is between two and four years.

Family Life: The Pack
Wolves are social creatures. Algonquin's wolves live in groups (packs). Pack size is usually between four and seven animals. Each pack has a leader who is the strongest and largest wolf. The lines of authority in a wolf community are very clear: each wolf is subordinate to those that are bigger and stronger than it is. Each pack has its own territory in which they are the only wolves that hunt. In Algonquin Park, this territory can be as large as 500 to 600 km^2. The wolves mark their territory by urinating on trees along its borders.

Family Life: The Young
Each wolf pack supports only one mating pair. The pack's dominant male and female mate near the end of each winter and produce one litter of four to six pups in the spring. The wolf mother gives birth in a den, dug into a hill, which is accessible only through a tunnel. She stays in the den with the pups for two weeks and does not allow any other wolf to enter. The birth of the pups becomes the focus of life in the wolf pack. The lead male drops off food at the head of the tunnel for the mother and the others wait for the pups to emerge. For the first three months of their lives, the young wolves sleep in the den each night, and are nursed with their mother's milk. When they are able to eat meat, all members of the pack help to feed them by providing the meat, which they ingest at the place of the kill and later regurgitate, for the pups at the den. All wolves take turns playing with the young and teaching them games like pouncing on sticks and play-fighting. Such games teach hunting skills and help to establish the young wolves' places in the pack's line of authority. By the fall, the young pups have learned to catch and eat frogs and mice. They are able to take part in the pack's hunting excursions by late fall.

This photo was taken during one of the most amazing wolf encounters I have ever experienced. An aquaintance and I were floating in a canoe on one of the many small lakes along Highway 60, when we saw something move in the distance. This wolf walked around the shore toward us, stopped directly in front of us (no more than 15 m away) and took a drink from the lake before walking off into the forest.

When and How to See a Wolf

Wolves are one of the most difficult of Algonquin's animals to see. If you are lucky enough to see a wolf, you may count yourself among a small group of fortunate people. Driving "the circuit", as described in the animal watching section of the *Activities* chapter, remains the best option; an early morning walk on the Mizzy Lake Trail may also be fruitful. Although they are seldom seen, you stand a good chance of hearing their magical and unforgettable wild howls. A wolf howl is a timeless sound that can make the hair stand up on the back of your neck. Listening to it amid the beauty of the Algonquin forests is an unforgettable experience. Wolves howl for a variety of reasons: to inform other packs trespassing in their territory that they are not welcome or to find their way back to the pack should they become separated at night. Human vocal cords are capable of producing a howl that sounds remarkably similar to that of a wolf. Consequently, wolves often respond to human attempts at howling.

Public Wolf Howls

Park naturalists conduct Public Wolf Howls once a week in the month of August when they successfully locate a pack of wolves in the wild. They take up to 2000 people to a nearby point along the highway and proceed to howl; 70% of the time the wolves howl back! It is an eerie and truly wild experience. Visitors in the Park during August should enquire with Park staff at the Visitor Centre or at either of the Gates as to when the next Howl will take place.

Further Interest:

- *Wolf Howling In Algonquin Provincial Park** Park Technical Bulletin number #3, $0.75 – why wolves howl, how public wolf howls came to be popular in Algonquin, tips on how to try howling on your own.
- Amazing recordings of howling wolves can be found on *Voices of Algonquin Park**, a cassette narrated by Ron Tozer who explains the reasons behind the howls.
- *The Howls of August – Encounters with Algonquin's Wolves*. Mike Runtz. Boston Mills Publishing Erin, Ont, 1997.
- *The Wolf*. David Mech. Natural History Press. New York. 1970.
- *Wolf Country: 11 Years Tracking Algonquin Wolves*. John B. Theberge. McClelland & Steward, 1998, - the product of one of the longest-running wolf studies in North America.

9.8

ROBERT BATEMAN
Gray Jay Study
Gouache

GRAY JAY
(Perisoreus canadensis)

Weight:	68 – 82 g
Length (including tail):	27 – 31 cm
Wingspan:	38 – 43 cm
Diet:	Omnivore
Chance of seeing:	Good from Aug to mid-Oct, Very good from mid-Oct to Mar, Slim from Mar to Aug

Appearance: Loose, fluffy plumage, small billed, long tailed.
Usually seen in groups of three.

Markings: Dull, dark or brownish-grey upper parts.
Light grey to white underparts.
Whitish face and throat.

About the Gray Jay

In many ways, the fascinating lives of Gray Jays are exceptions to the norms of the bird world. Highly-developed food stashing practices allow them to stay in their northern territories during the winter while other birds undertake long migratory voyages. They have a well-earned reputation for boldness, having been observed landing on the backs of live moose to capture tasty winter ticks, and upon human hands to take food. They are known by a variety of different names including Canada Jay and the old woodsman term Whiskey Jack. Whiskey Jack is a derivitive of *"wiskédjak"* - its Native American name, which indicated a belief that it was the embodiment of a spirit. Algonquin Park, which lies near the southern limit of its eastern range, has been the home of serious enquiry into Gray Jay biology and behaviour for over 30 years. Much of the following information was gathered from the Algonquin study.

What Gray Jays Eat

Gray Jays could never be accused of being fussy eaters! They catch a wide range of insects including spiders, caterpillars and beetles. Keen foragers, they search for all sorts of berries, mushrooms and other fungi; they also take small pieces of meat from dead fish, birds, bears and smaller mammals. They commonly take eggs and nestlings, and occasionally catch and kill mice. Gray Jays establish territories, which, from a series of perches, they survey almost continuously for food. Studies of Algonquin Park Gray Jays have found the average size of their territories to be roughly 1.5 km^2.

Predators

Red Squirrels and the Broad-winged Hawk, which is Algonquin's most common bird of prey, take nestlings, while the Northern Goshawk and Merlin are each known to snatch mature Gray Jays. Gray Jays alert each other to the presence of threats by a whistled alarm note. Common strategies employed to discourage predators include bristling their head feathers to create a larger than life appearance, and banding together to mob flying intruders or dive-bomb those on the ground. The oldest reported Gray Jay in the wild was an Algonquin Park female that was last seen when it was 16 years old.

Winter

Winter is the most difficult time of the year for almost all bird species found in Algonquin Park. It is accompanied by high rates of death. Cold temperatures and a deep blanket of snow greatly reduce the amount of food available to the Park's birds. The vast majority cope by migrating long distances to warmer ecosystems. The loon flies to the waters off the southern USA, while the bobolink travels all the way to Argentina! Only a few hearty bird species remain in the Park. In each case, they have a highly specialized strategy to overcome the hardships of the harsh winter. The Gray Jay's approach involves storing food for winter consumption. Long summer days are spent collecting insects, berries, mushrooms and meat. Each treat is coated in sticky saliva and then stuck behind a flake of tree bark or under a tuft of lichen for later retrieval. Perhaps future studies will reveal that their glue-like saliva contains a preservative or antibacterial agent that delays the decomposition of these stored items. By the time the first flakes of snow start falling in late November, successful Gray Jays have stashed food in thousands of locations. Amazingly enough, their tiny "bird brains" direct them back to these locations throughout the entire winter! This method works so well that studies done in Algonquin Park have found that Gray Jays are less likely to die in the harsh winter than in the carefree days of summer. Furthermore, their average yearly mortality rate of 18% is far below the 50% loss that many migratory birds experience.

Family Life and Early Development

Gray Jays are true homebodies. They mate for life, remain in the same territory 12 months of the year and rarely stray out of earshot of their mate. In fact, these closely bonded birds use "peeps" to remain in constant contact with their partner while they are temporarily away on food storage trips. Gray Jay couples breed yearly, building a new nest in Black Spruce or Balsam Fir trees in late February or early March. The breeding pair constructs their nest together, travelling to and from the site in tandem fashion. The female lays her clutch, most commonly of three eggs, in early March amid temperatures that can plummet to –30 °C. Such behaviour is

Wayne Van Sickle

In the winter months, Gray Jays will often take food from an outstretched hand.

extremely rare in the local bird community; most species wait until the warm food-rich months of May and June. Unlike loon couples who share the job of incubating their eggs, the female Gray Jay performs that role exclusively. She sits on her eggs for 20 days, leaving the nest every 3 to 4 hours for just a few minutes. The young hatch in mid-April, open their eyes roughly 10 days later and fly from the nest when they are 21 to 23 days old. They have been seen picking up food for themselves two or three weeks later, and engaging in food stashing behaviour a few days later. Despite this quick learning curve, they are unable to gather enough food on their own for their first winter, and therefore require access to the parental stash. However, Gray Jay couples apparently gather only enough food to ensure the survival of one additional family member. For whatever reason, the dominant youngster drives its siblings out of the family territory in mid-June (roughly two months into life) and is thereby assured exclusive access to the parental food subsidy. Expelled youngsters attempt to join unsuccessful breeding couples who will tolerate their presence. Regardless of whether the young spend the winter with natural or adoptive parents, they are driven from the territory before the onset of the next breeding season. Most Gray Jays breed for the first time in their second year.

How to Spot a Gray Jay

The two biggest factors that affect the chances of encountering Gray Jays are time of year and forest type. Many of Algonquin's Gray Jays have learned to regard humans as sources of new food and consequently become very friendly in times of limited food availability. In late fall and throughout winter, visitors are commonly approached by Gray Jays who are willing to be seen at close range. At these times of the year, visitors stand a good chance of enticing the birds to land on open hands full of nuts, raisins and little pieces of cheese or bread. However, the warmer months of the year tell a very different story, Gray Jays have no problems finding their own food and therefore they have little use for humans and are spotted much less frequently. Gray Jays inhabit coniferous forests, especially preferring low-lying Black Spruce bogs. They are sometimes found in mixed forests, beaver meadows and clearings, but they almost totally avoid areas dominated by the Sugar Maple. Prime viewing areas located along Highway 60 include:

- Opeongo Road at km 46.3 – especially the north half of the 6 km road
- Mizzy Lake Day Hiking Trail at km 15.4
- Spruce Bog Boardwalk Trail at km 42.5

If walks in these areas are not fruitful, visitors are encouraged to stop in at the Visitor Centre and ask for the locations of recent sightings.

The Ongoing Gray Jay Study

A well-known Park Naturalist, by the name of Russell J. Rutter, began studying Algonquin's Gray Jays in the 1960's. He passed away in 1976, but not before he had sparked the interest of Dan Strickland, who is now Algonquin's Chief Park Naturalist. Dan has kept many aspects of Rutter's study alive, and has also done considerable work to increase our understanding of the complex relationship between Gray Jay behaviour and social organization.

- *Colour Banding*

Identifying individual birds is the first step toward understanding their species. Identification allows for the tracking of birds over time and for the meaningful observation of an individual's behaviour. This is achieved in the Algonquin Gray Jay Study, as it is in many long-term bird studies, by banding. Strickland locates Gray Jay nests and monitors their progress throughout February and

March. He places three coloured bands (in addition to a plain aluminum band refered to as "Standard") on any nestling surviving to the 11th day mark. Unique combinations allow for visual identification throughout the bird's lifetime without recapture. At any one time there are between 30 and 35 pairs of banded adults in the Park, in addition to numerous unattached youngsters. Reaching the nests is not always an easy task. Nests can be located in difficult to reach places, up to 15 m above the ground. A ladder doesn't always provide access, and in the past, Dan has had to build scaffolding, and come up with other inventive techniques just to reach the nest!

- *The Annual Fall Round-up*

Gray Jays are elusive and difficult to encounter in the summer. Dan catches up with the birds in the fall. He visits each Gray Jay territory in the study area to see which birds are present. Rather than conduct an exhaustive search of each territory, he erects suet feeders in easily accessible locations, and returns the following day after the birds have discovered them. In such a manner, he is able to visit 25 to 30 territories in a day or two and identify the birds present, as well as catch and band any new individual which has replaced a previous occupant over the summer.

How Visitors Can Help With The Gray Jay Study

New understandings will undoubtedly grow out of continuing research. Visitors can make valuable contributions to the study by reporting any sighting of a banded Gray Jay, at any time of the year. The birds are identified not only by the colours of the four bands on their legs, but also by which leg they appear on, and in what order. A bird whose left leg has a white band above a purple one, and whose right leg has an orange band over a standard aluminum band can be identified as WOPLOOSR (**W**hite **O**ver **P**urple **L**eft, **O**range **O**ver **S**tandard **R**ight). The study uses ten colours, including both light and dark shades of blue and green. It is best to write the complicated colour pattern down on paper. Reports of sightings, along with their location, can be dropped off, to the attention of Dan Strickland, at either of the Highway 60 Gates or at the Visitor Centre. As a thank you for assisting in the study, Dan will send a record of the bird's history to anyone who includes a mailing address with his or her sighting.

=9.9=

Chris Boettger

BLACK BEAR
(Ursus americanus)

Weight:	70 - 150 kg (male)
	55 - 120 kg (female)
Head and body length:	150 - 180 cm
Diet:	Omnivore
Chance of seeing:	Low

About the Black Bear

North America is home to several types of bears. Those found in Algonquin Park are known as Black Bears. Canada's Black Bear population is estimated to be approximately 400,000. Between 75,000 and 100,000 are found in Ontario. Despite the fact that Algonquin's Black Bears can weigh up to 150 kg, they are smaller than both the legendary Grizzly Bear, which is found to the west of the Canadian Rocky Mountains, and the Polar Bear, which is found in Canada's Far North. Park naturalists estimate that there are as many as 2,000 Black Bears in Algonquin Park. Despite the potential for harm, there have been very few bear attacks in the Park. Each year roughly 400,000 people visit the Park and avoid confrontations with bears by following the simple rules listed at the end of this chapter.

Physical Characteristics

Black Bears are multi-talented animals, and if there were an animal equivalent of the Olympics, they just might win the decathlon! They can run at speeds of up to 50 km/h and swim across small lakes and rivers with ease. They are also master tree climbers. Black Bears have razor-sharp claws and amazing strength, which enables them to shake small trees and overturn large rocks. It's easy to see how they might win the gold medal. Bears have keen senses of hearing and smell. A bear's nose is its best friend. It tells him all he needs to know about what or whom he meets in the forest. Often a bear will stand up on his hind legs when it encounters a person or animal in the forest. This practice is widely misunderstood as a sign of aggression; in reality, it simply helps the bear to get a better sense of what or whom it has encountered.

What a Bear Eats

Black Bears will eat just about anything they can find – plant or animal. A Black Bear's diet changes greatly with the seasons and the availability of certain foods. In the spring, when there is little else available, they usually eat grass. By June, tree leaves quickly become the staple of their diet. They are especially fond of leaves from the Aspen Tree. Such *hors d'oeuvres* merely wet their appetite for summer's main course - berries. Black Bears spend the long days of summer picking blueberries and raspberries with their long, soft tongues, which curl around the berry and pull it off the bush. They also enjoy seeds of all kinds, roots, acorns, grasshoppers, beetles, grubs, turtles, wasps, salamanders and fish, as well as young moose and deer. Bears are fond of honey, knocking over beehives in order to lick out the sweet gold. They need not worry about being stung because their thick hair protects them from the bee's sting.

To ensure an adequate food supply, Algonquin's Black Bears claim part of the Park as their own, and defend it against any other bear that might wander into it. Depending on the size of the bear, and the availability of food in the area, these territories can be anywhere from 10 to 140 km^2 in size. They mark their territory by standing up on their back legs and cutting into the bark of trees with their claws. Other bears can see how big the bear is by noting how high up on the tree the marks are; a bigger bear commands more respect and therefore a larger territory.

A Bear's Enemies
An adult black bear in Algonquin Park has little to fear. No animal poses any threat to it whatsoever. The danger of predation exists only when the bear is young. It sounds unbelievable, but a male Black Bear will kill and devour any unprotected young bears that he may come across - including his own! The mother bear is very protective of her cubs for that very reason, and will aggressively fight off any creature that comes too close. If a bear survives its childhood, it may live as long as 10 to 15 years.

A Winter's Sleep
Food is scarce during the long cold winter, so bears sleep the season away in a state of hibernation. Many animals, including bats and ground hogs, hibernate. Although each experiences reductions in heart rate, breathing rate, and body temperature, there appears to be different degrees of hibernation. Ground hogs undergo significant reductions, have very little bodily functions, and are next to impossible to rouse from their sleep. The Black Bear's hibernation involves relatively minor decreases in blood pressure and breathing rate and a drop of only a few degrees in body temperature. In this state from which they are easily roused, bears get nourishment from a thick layer of fat that builds up, thanks to late summer feasting and gorging sessions in the fall where, literally, they eat all day long. In addition to putting on a layer of fat, bears grow an extra thick coat of fur to keep them warm in temperatures that may drop to below -30° C. Black Bears do not defecate or urinate during

hibernation; in fact, their urine is recycled by their systems. Bears pass the winter in dens. In Algonquin, dens can be located under logs, stumps or among the roots of trees. Yellow Birch trees provide many ideal sites. Their seeds have a difficult time reaching the soil through the thick layer of Sugar Maple leaves, which cover forest floors. Many Yellow Birches succeed only when their seeds fall on top of an old rotting stump. Their roots grow around the stump and down into the ground. Park naturalists affectionately refer to such a stump as a "Perched Birch". Years later, when the stump rots away, the Yellow Birch roots remain in place - a little digging turns the site into prime denning material.

Family Life

The adult male and female bear do not live together, nor do they associate with each other, except at mating time, when they come together only briefly to copulate. Afterwards they go their separate ways. The male takes no part whatsoever in the rearing of his offspring. A female bear mates every second summer. There is a delayed implantation of her eggs for three to four months so that her litter of two to three young will be born in midwinter while she is in her deep sleep. The cubs nurse throughout the winter and are ready to leave the den with their mother in May to learn hunting and foraging skills. They will remain with their mother throughout the summer and spend the next winter with her in her den. By the following spring they are ready to strike out on their own.

Bear Etiquette and Precautions

1) Never feed a bear: to do so is to kill it and put fellow campers in danger. Experience shows that bears fed by humans learn to associate campers with food and may stroll into campgrounds looking for food. Park rangers will attempt to relocate such bears but will have to shoot those that keep coming back.

2) Never bring any food, food wrappers or other scented items such as toothpaste or perfume into your tent. Bears have no interest in people. They're interested only in their food. If you don't have any food in your tent, chances are you won't have a bear in there either!

3) Ensure that your campsite is kept clean at all times, burn any burnable garbage and dispose of the rest in the bear-proof garbage cans found in the campgrounds and throughout the Park. Never leave food or dirty dishes about.

Black bears are tree climbers; campers must secure their edibles.

4) Place all food and scented items securely in your vehicle so bears are not tempted to visit your site. Those camped in the interior, or those without a car, should place such items, as well as non-burnable garbage, in a bag or pack suspended by rope from a large tree branch. The bag must hang at least 4 m (13 feet) off the ground and 2 m (6 ½ feet) away from the tree trunk.

Where and How to See a Bear
Despite large numbers, Park visitors rarely see bears. Bears have remarkable senses of hearing and smell, and tend to disappear long before people see them. Sighting a bear in the forest or along a trail is a chance occurrence.

- The best method is to drive "the circuit" as described in the animal watching section of the *Activities* chapter and hope for a rare encounter.
- Bears are occasionally seen from the viewing platform at the Visitor Centre during the summer berry season. Free-use telescopes are mounted on the deck.
- Mounted black bears are on permanent display at the Visitor Centre.

10.1

Wayne Van Sickle

WHISKEY RAPIDS TRAIL

Location:	Hwy 60 at km 7.2
Trail length:	2.1 km
Difficulty:	Easy
Avg hiking time:	1 hr & 30 min

Highlights:

- Rated as one of the easier trails along the Highway 60 Corridor.
- Travels along the banks of an Algonquin river.
- Visits scenic rapids.

Concerns:

- The trail can be difficult to follow.
- Mud abounds in May and early June.

About the Trail

Much of this easy-to-hike trail follows the shoreline of the pretty Oxtongue River. The Oxtongue River is one of eight major Ontario rivers that find their start in the Park. These eight rivers played important roles throughout history. Native Americans used them as canoe routes linking traditional hunting grounds. They were also important transportation routes for trappers who paddled the rivers in canoes weighted down by beaver and other animal pelts. Less than 100 years ago, these rivers were also used by loggers who floated timber downstream to larger rivers, and ultimately to mighty ships that sailed overseas to British markets. The protection of the headwaters of these eight rivers was also one of the reasons for the creation of Algonquin Park in 1893. The trail booklet visits some of these historical themes as well as discusses Algonquin River ecology, from algae to Black Flies and Kingfishers. The booklet also recounts the story of how an ill-fated celebration of loggers, at the close of the 1800's, provided the rapids with their name.

Over the years, birders have found the Whiskey Rapids Trail to be a good location for spotting Spruce Grouse, Black-backed Woodpecker, Boreal Chickadee, Brown Creepers and Northern Parula.

A word to the wise - pay close attention to the trail during your hike. I've lost my way on more than one occasion and have had to resort to finding my own way back to the parking lot.

10.2

Wayne Van Sickle

HARDWOOD
LOOKOUT TRAIL

Location:	Hwy 60 at km 13.8
Trail length:	0.8 km
Difficulty:	Moderate
Avg hiking time:	45 min

Highlights:
- A scenic lookout over a large lake.
- Bright wildflowers in early spring.
- Spectacular red, gold and orange trees in the fall.

Concerns:
- Steep cliffs.

About the Trail

This trail winds its way through a hardwood forest dominated by Maple trees. Most everyone, young or old, can conquer the short, but steep, walking incline to the trail's lookout point. Once there, a few benches made from felled trees provide excellent places to catch your breath and take in the view. A large body of water called Smoke Lake is visible through a clearing in the trees. Although the trail is well worth the walk at any time of the year, it is especially stunning in the spring and the fall.

Thousands of wildflowers bloom in Algonquin's hardwood forests in early May. Bright yellow flowers known as Trout Lilies (*Erythronium americanum - see pg 19*) appear first, followed by smaller white and pink flowers called Northern Spring-Beauties (*Claytonia caroliniana*) and by the larger Red Trillium (*Trillium erectum - see pg 42*). Most of these colourful wildflowers have disappeared by late May or early June, when the Maple trees above them sprout leaves and block out the sun.

Each fall, the leaves of the Sugar Maple tree give up their bright green appearance and take on a golden yellow hue which later gives way to orange and bright scarlet. As the trees change colours at slightly different paces, they light up Algonquin's hills and perform an unforgettable symphony of colour. The Hardwood Lookout Trail is one of the best places along Highway 60 to view this amazing spectacle.

Although the Hardwood Lookout Trail is not usually a good place to see Algonquin's larger mammals, it can be productive for birders. The forest is a good location for spotting Yellow-bellied Sapsuckers, Pileated Woodpeckers, Eastern Wood-Pewees, Least Flycatchers, Wood Thrushes, Scarlet Tanagers and Barred Owls.

10.3

Wayne Van Sickle

MIZZY LAKE TRAIL

Location:	Highway 60 at km 15.4
Trail length:	11 km
Difficulty:	Moderate
Avg hiking time:	5 hr

Highlights:
- #1 ranked trail for wildlife encounters.

ABOUT THE TRAIL

The Mizzy Lake Trail is relatively flat. It visits nine small ponds and lakes. In between, it passes through dark Algonquin forests, low-lying wet areas and small stream habitats. Portions of the trail are board-walked for easier passage. In terms of animal watching, the Mizzy Lake Trail stands head and shoulders above the other day hiking trails located along the Highway 60 Corridor. In fact, it was specifically designed for encountering Algonquin's animals, especially moose!

In the summer, moose are frequently seen standing in the shallow lakes and ponds along both sides of the trail, as they feast on aquatic plants. Numerous beaver dams and lodges can also be seen from the trail. Hikers stand a good chance of seeing the beavers themselves, especially if they heed the beaver-spotting tips found earlier in the *Beaver* chapter. Painted turtles are often seen sunning themselves on the partially submerged logs found in several of the trailside ponds. The most productive portions of the trail occur roughly halfway into the 11 km, five hour hike. Starting early with the sunrise is the best way to increase the odds of a rewarding encounter.

Birders should concentrate their efforts in the Wolf Howl Pond and West Rose Lake vicinities (see the map in the Mizzy Lake Trail booklet which is available at the trailhead). Park naturalists have found these areas to be good for American Bittern, Wood Duck, Ring-necked Duck, Hooded Merganser, Spruce Grouse, Common Snipe, Black-backed Woodpecker, Olive-sided Flycatcher, Yellow-bellied Flycatcher, Alder Flycatcher, Boreal Chickadee, Winter Wren and Lincoln's Sparrow.

The trail is notorious for muddy sections; hikers should be prepared to get a little dirty.

10.4

Wayne Van Sickle

PECK LAKE TRAIL

Location:	Hwy 60 at km 19.2
Trail length:	1.9 km
Difficulty:	Easy to moderate
Avg hiking time:	45 min

Highlights:

- An opportunity to walk completely around an Algonquin lake.
- The potential to see loons and other waterfowl.

About the Trail

Lakes are the defining feature of the Algonquin landscape and one of the main reasons many animals, including the loon are able to make their home in the Park. Loons and other Park animals couldn't exist in Algonquin without productive food chains. In fact, each adult loon requires up to 1 kg of fish each day. Although Algonquin's lakes can sometimes appear peaceful and still, there is always plenty of action taking place under their surface. The trail guide-booklet describes the amazing interconnecting web of species and processes that occur in Algonquin's lakes.

Over the years, Peck Lake has been home to loons that have built their nests along its shorelines and spent the summer raising their young. The trail travels all the way around the small lake. If the lake's wildlife is active when you visit, you'll likely get a good view.

After completing the walk, some hikers head over to the Visitor Centre, where they can view a great exhibit regarding the food chain of the Park's lakes.

10.5

Wayne Van Sickle

TRACK AND
TOWER TRAIL

Location:	Hwy 60 at km 25
Trail length:	7.7 km (main loop trail)
Difficulty:	Strenuous due to steep climbs
Avg hiking time:	3 hr & 30 min

Highlights:
- A spectacular lookout.
- Scenic streams, ponds and lakes.
- A man-made dam.
- The remains of an historic railroad line.

Concerns:
- Old bush roads, canoe route portages, shortcuts and a 5.5 km side-trail cross the main trail at various points. Hikers who don't pay close attention to the map included in the guide booklet (available at the trailhead) may become lost.
- Steep cliffs.

About the Trail

I find the Track and Tower Trail to be one of Algonquin's most rewarding and enjoyable trails. It passes by numerous natural and man-made places of interest. Hikers visit picturesque streams, small waterfalls and peaceful lakes while travelling through some of the prettiest forests in the Park. It is a good place to see a variety of birds, including Scarlet Tanagers, that breed in the area. Moose have also been known to frequent the area. Without a doubt, one of the highlights of the trail is the expansive view of the forest and Cache Lake below. The trail travels across a few wooden bridges, which are great places to take photographs. It also visits a man made dam, as well as the remains of railway bridges that were constructed 100 years ago to transport timber logged in the Park.

The Algonquin railroad was once one of the busiest tracks in Canada. Reports from the early 1900's say that a train went by every ten minutes! The area surrounding the trail was the site of much human activity in the early 1900's. At one point, there was even a luxury hotel with over 100 rooms on the shores of Cache Lake.

You would probably never guess, if it wasn't pointed out to you, but portions of the quiet, green trail follow the path of the old railroad. The trail booklet, entitled "A Look into Algonquin's Past", draws hikers attention to the sites of former activity. It makes use of sketches and old photographs to portray the past.

10.6

Wayne Van Sickle

HEMLOCK BLUFF TRAIL

Location:	Hwy 60 at km 27.2
Trail length:	3.5 km
Difficulty:	Easy
Avg hiking time:	1 hr & 30 min

Highlights:

- A pleasant lookout point above a quiet lake.
- Easy walking.

Concerns

- Unlike the other trails, the Hemlock Bluff trail starts across the highway from the parking lot.

About the Trail

Among the trail's best features are the large Hemlock trees that keep the forest dark and cool, even on the hottest of days. It is one of the best places to escape the hot summer sun. A number of bird species pass through, or make their homes in the area, including Yellow-bellied Sapsucker, Brown Creeper, Winter Wren, Golden-crowned Kinglet, Swainson's Thrush, Hermit Thrush, Northern Parula, Black-throated Green Warbler and Blackburnian Warbler.

The trail itself rises gradually through a mixed hardwood and Eastern Hemlock forest, to a lookout point above a quiet lake. The lookout point is not as spectacular as those found on some of the other trails (see Trail Ranking Chart), but it is nevertheless quite memorable. It is also a good place to enjoy a packed lunch. A flight of wooden stairs facilitates the descent from the lookout point to the lake below. Before returning to the highway, the trail travels along the rugged and rocky shore of Jack Lake.

The trail's guide booklet introduces the hiker to the rich scientific research history of Algonquin Park. Algonquin has been described as the single most important area in Canada for biological research. The booklet presents a sampling of the broad range of studies conducted on the Park's flora and fauna.

10.7

Wayne Van Sickle

BAT LAKE
TRAIL

Location:	Hwy 60 at km 30
Trail length:	5.6 km
Difficulty:	Easy
Avg hiking time:	2 hr & 30 min

Highlights:

- A wide variety of scenery.
- A smooth, easy to hike trail.
- A boardwalk out into a small lake.
- A naturally acidic lake.

About the Trail:

The Bat Lake Trail is one of the Park's mid length trails. Although it is longer than many, at 5.6 km, it is a relatively easy hike because the trail is flat and mostly smooth. It also tends to be quieter than many of the shorter trails, which are hiked by far more people. The strength of this trail lies in its variety.

The trail starts out through a softwood forest populated by Pine, Cedar and Spruce, but soon enters into a deciduous forest dominated by the Sugar Maple tree. Later on, the trail brings hikers into a Black Spruce and Tamarack forest. This changing territory is a fine demonstration of the fact that Algonquin Park is located in the transitional forest zone of North America. Deciduous (hardwood) trees increasingly dominate forests to the South of the Park, while the forests to the north are largely comprised of coniferous (softwood) trees. The trail also visits bogs and pleasant streams. A 10 metre boardwalk takes hikers out onto a small lake that is 25 times more acidic than most of the lakes found in Algonquin. The trail booklet examines the history of this naturally acidic lake and offers a look at the unusual creatures living within and around it.

The opportunity to spot wildlife is also present along this trail. Park naturalists recommend that birders try its mixed forest for Spruce Grouse, Black-backed Woodpecker, Gray Jay, Boreal Chickadee, Winter Wren, Golden-crowned Kinglet and several warblers. The forest floor is busy with the activity of countless chipmunks. I have even heard report of Black Bear sightings along the trail.

10.8

Renee Gorrell

TWO RIVERS TRAIL

Location:	Hwy 60 at km 31
Trail length:	2.1 km
Difficulty:	Easy to moderate
Avg hiking time:	30 min

Highlights:
- An easy ascent to a lookout point above a scenic river.
- Relatively quick hiking time.

Concerns:
- Steep cliffs.

About the Trail

The Two Rivers Hiking Trail is arguably the best option for those wishing to hike to a rewarding lookout point without exerting too much time and energy. The footpath is less rugged than many of the other trails found along the Highway 60 Corridor. The lookout point provides impressive views of the meandering North Madawaska River and of the forests at its banks. It is a fine destination to enjoy a packed lunch.

The Checklist and Seasonal Status of the Birds of Algonquin Provincial Park lists this trail as one of the 15 recommended birding areas along Highway 60. Hikers may see Black-backed Woodpecker, Gray Jay, Boreal Chickadee, Golden-crowned Kinglet, and several species of warblers including Cape May Warbler.

The Two Rivers Trail guide-booklet, which is available at the trailhead, discusses the effects of logging, fire, insects and other man-made and natural forces which have been known to change the look of Algonquin's forests.

10.9

Wayne Van Sickle

CENTENNIAL RIDGES TRAIL

Location:	2 km drive from Hwy 60 at km 37.6
Trail length:	10 km
Difficulty:	Very strenuous due to steep climbs and trail length
Avg hiking time:	6 hr

Highlights:

- The best trail along the Highway 60 Corridor in terms of scenic views.
- Several beaver ponds.

Concerns:

- Numerous steep cliffs
- Constant rises and descents make this long trail very physically demanding

About the Trail

This lengthy trail travels along two high ridge systems. Roughly one-half of the trail follows the exposed ridgeline, while the other half winds through forests and around picturesque beaver ponds. Hikers repeatedly tackle significant inclines to reach high cliffs. In total, the trail visits five cliffs. At one point, hikers are 170 m above the trailhead. The expansive views over deep blue lakes, forested islands and rolling hills are stunning. Centennial Ridges is by far the most demanding of the walking trails described in this book. Hikers will appreciate each of the seven lookout points for the opportunity to catch their breath, as much as for the amazing views they provide.

The trail was blazed in 1993 to celebrate Algonquin Park's 100th year anniversary. The trail's guide booklet presents a look at the contributions and passions of 14 historical figures associated with the Park during its first 100 years. The diverse list includes the Park's founders, two early Park Superintendents, a Park ranger, wildlife biologists and an artist.

Although challenging, this trail is within the grasp of any person who is in good physical condition and has the time to take it slowly. If you are up for a workout, I can't imagine a more rewarding way to spend a day!

10.10

Wayne Van Sickle

LOOKOUT
TRAIL

Location:	Highway 60 at km 39.7
Trail length:	1.9 km
Difficulty:	Moderate to strenuous
Avg hiking time:	45 min

Highlights:
- One of the best lookout points in the Park.
- Bright wildflowers in early May.
- A stunning place to view the fall colours.

Concerns:
- Steep cliffs.

About the Trail

Hikers reach the lookout point, high atop the rocky cliffs, after a moderate to strenuous walking ascent through a hardwood forest. The view from the cliffs at Post 4 is among the most impressive in the Park. On a clear day visibility can be as great as 25 km. Hikers look out over a great expanse of forest and can see three blue lakes off in the distance. There is plenty of room on the cliffs to walk about or to simply lie down and bathe in the sun. I have arrived at the lookout more than once to find entire wedding parties being photographed on the rocks. Some couples even choose to have the ceremony performed here! The view is awe-inspiring at any time of the year, but is especially stunning during the peak of the fall colours, when the sprawling forests below are spread out like a giant red carpet. In late April or May, thousands of bright yellow and red wildflowers sprout up from the forest floor.

The chances of spotting any of Algonquin's larger mammals along the trail are poor, but birding enthusiasts can look for Hermit Thrush and Dark-eyed Junco. Broad-winged Hawks can sometimes be spotted from the cliffs. Although short, the trail is quite rugged. The footpath is dotted with exposed tree roots, which can easily trip hikers if they aren't careful. The numbered posts along the trail and the accompanying educational trail booklet are designed to provide hikers with an introduction to the geology of Algonquin Park.

Enjoy the view from the lookout, but don't get too close to the edge of the cliff. It is 125 m above the lakes below!

10.11

Wayne Van Sickle

BOOTH'S ROCK TRAIL

Location:	8 km drive from Highway 60 at km 40.3
Trail length:	5.1 km
Difficulty:	Strenuous
Avg hiking time:	3 hr

Highlights:
- One of the top three lookouts among the day-hiking trails.
- Remains of an old estate and railway.
- Several quiet lakes.

Concerns:
- Steep cliffs

About the Trail

This is my favourite trail in Algonquin Park. It is the perfect length for an afternoon of wandering. Part of the trail follows an old railway line that was once among the busiest in the country. Today, the area is peaceful and full of nature. The trail travels through dense forests and along the shores of two pretty lakes. There are several wonderful places to take breaks in the sun or even enjoy a quick swim. The lookout point is located on a cliff high above Rock Lake. Hikers are treated to an exciting panoramic view of the lake, several islands and the great forest below. The view is unobstructed for 180 degrees.

The trail also provides a glimpse into the past. The trail-booklet leads hikers to the remains of an estate once occupied by a powerful judge. All that remains today are several building foundations, a huge cement dock and an overgrown tennis court upon which the lines can still be seen.

To access the trail, turn south onto the Rock Lake Road at km 40.3. Follow the signs marked Booth's Rock Trail. The dirt road travels 8 km before passing through the Rock Lake campground and eventually reaching the small parking lot for the trail. Not only is the drive along the short road a welcome change from the busy paved highway, but it also passes through some beautiful territory. Fisher Lake, just off the east side of the road, is particularly scenic. I often go there to think, or just take in the view. The steep and rocky cliffs reflect on the lake's surface on calm mornings and evenings. Those looking closely at the cliffs will be able to pick out the location of a raven's nest by the large white stains on the rock face below it. Beavers have been active in the area and I have also encountered moose in the vicinity.

10.12

Wayne Van Sickle

SPRUCE BOG
BOARDWALK

Location:	Highway 60 at km 42.5
Trail length:	1.5 km
Difficulty:	Easy
Avg hiking time:	30 min

Highlights:
- Easy walking territory.
- The opportunity to explore an environment not normally accessible by foot.
- Ground that appears to be solid but is actually unable to support your weight.
- One of the best places in the region to witness the courtship ritual of the Spruce Grouse in April and May.

About the Trail

The Spruce Bog Boardwalk is rated as the easiest of the day-hiking trails found along the Highway 60 Corridor. It is relatively flat and one-half of it is planked boardwalk. The boardwalk allows hikers to enter a very wet environment (known as a bog) that is not normally accessible by foot. Bogs are areas that are in the lengthy transitional process from a lake environment to that of a forest. The guide-booklet, which is available at the trailhead, describes the steps that occur in this transformation. Numbered posts along the trail point out places in different stages of the process. One such area looks like solid ground, but is really a thin layer of plants floating atop a deep pond filled with acidic water.

Local bird expert Ron Tozer considers the Spruce Bog Boardwalk to offer the "most accessible birding for northern species along Highway 60". The forests may contain Spruce Grouse, Olive-sided Flycatcher, Yellow-bellied Flycatcher, Gray Jay, Boreal Chickadee and Hermit Thrush, while the creek and bog may yield American Bittern, Ring-necked Duck, Northern Harrier, Sedge Wren and Lincoln's Sparrow.

In my opinion, the Spruce Bog Boardwalk is the most unique trail in the Park. It is well worth the 30 minutes that it takes to walk it. After completing the walk, many visitors retire to the Visitor Centre across the highway to enjoy a drink in its cafeteria and enjoy the view from the observation deck.

10.13

Wayne Van Sickle

BEAVER POND
TRAIL

Location:	Highway 60 at km 45.2
Trail length:	2.0 km
Difficulty:	Moderate
Avg hiking time:	1 hr & 15 min

Highlights:
- See beaver dams and lodges up close.
- Potential for sighting beaver and moose.
- A lookout point that demonstrates the beaver's impact on its environment.

Concerns:
- Steep cliffs.

About the Trail

As the name of the trail indicates, the beaver is the theme of this interesting day-hike. Aside from man, no creature on the face of the Earth changes the environment as much as the beaver. Beavers cut down trees for nourishment and for use in the construction of their homes (lodges) and dams. Beaver dams turn small streams into large ponds or even lakes. This type of environmental change has major implications for the area's flora and fauna. This educational trail showcases the work of the large rodents. The educational guide-booklet, which is available at the trailhead, does a great job of discussing the consequences of beaver activity.

Beavers spend much of their lives in the water and have many unique physical features such as see-through eyelids, bright orange teeth and a second set of lips behind their teeth. Hikers will get close to beaver dams, lodges and perhaps even to the creatures themselves.

The trail is very rocky with frequent ascents and descents. Stairs have been constructed at some of the steepest places to aid hikers.

The Beaver Pond Trail is rated as the second best trail along Highway 60 for spotting wildlife. Apart from beavers, which will most commonly be seen in the evening, moose can be spotted in the shallow waters of Amikeus Lake. Wolves are also known to visit the area. Hikers may find it worthwhile to review the beaver chapter in this book either before they hike the trail or during the walk itself.

10.14

THOMSON, TOM
The Drive, c.1916. Oil on canvas.
Ontario Agriculture College purchase with funds raised by students, faculty and staff, 1926.
University of Guelph Collection

THE LOGGING MUSEUM TRAIL

Location: Hwy #60 at km 54.6
Level of difficulty: Easy
Trail length: 1.3 km
Hiking time: Between 1 and 2 hours.

Highlights:

- Easy, flat walking trail through a pine forest.
- Working log dam and chute.
- One of only three steam warping logging tugs left in the world.
- Reconstructed blacksmith shop with a separate booklet detailing the purpose of 78 tools.
- A ten minute film which recounts Algonquin's logging history.

About the Trail

Without a doubt this is the most sophisticated trail in the Park. In fact it is more than a trail, it is a first rate museum comprised of huge, antique and reconstructed exhibits placed outdoors along a wide, flat trail that cuts through a pleasant conifer forest.

Many people are surprised when they learn that logging is still permitted in Algonquin Park, but as anyone familiar with local history will tell you, loggers reached the area decades before anyone even thought of creating the great Park. They were present, even supportive, when the Park was formed in 1893 and have had a stake in it ever since. Today, Algonquin is the province's most important source of maple and pine logs. The Logging Museum provides insight into the fascinating history of Algonquin's logging industry and how it exists today inside what the world regards as one of its most cherished recreational "wilderness" areas.

A log reception building containing a history-orientated bookstore and three-dimensional pioneering logging displays (dioramas) is located at the trailhead. Visitors watch an informative audio-visual film in its theatre before walking the outdoor trail. The ten-minute film opens in the early 1800's with an account of the Napoleon blockade that cut England off from its traditional supply of ship building timber and ultimately led to the creation of Canada's logging industry. The film goes on to describe early logging practices and introduces many of the ingenious inventions that helped transform the face of logging throughout the last two centuries. At the conclusion of the film, which wraps up with a look at present-day logging in Algonquin, the screen rises for visitors to head outdoors where they pick up an excellent guide booklet and commence the easy self-guided walk between exhibits. It is entirely fitting that the loggers' stories are told in an outdoor setting, and with each step

A group of pioneer loggers. The log structure in the background is most likely a camboose shanty.

along the trail, visitors take a journey into the past. The first exhibit is a reconstructed dwelling known as a "camboose shanty" - a square log structure with a raised central fireplace in which up to 50 men spent the winter away from their families while they worked. The next few exhibits demonstrate how they cut, squared and dragged timber to frozen lakes, where it was left to wait for the swollen rivers of spring upon which it would later be floated all the way to ships waiting in far-off Quebec City.

The most ambitious exhibit is a life-size working reconstruction of a combination dam and log chute (similiar to the one pictured on title page of this section). Loggers used these structures to herd logs past rapids and other challenges. In this case, life-size means gigantic. The dam is actually functioning and has created a large pond, which, at time of writing, was complete with its own resident colony of beavers! Additional exhibits demonstrate how the intro-duction of the crosscut saw in the 1870's, and the Park railroad in 1896, changed the way loggers operated, and how 20th century in-ventions such as the two man chainsaw in the 1940's and the skidder in the 1950's continued to modernize the logging industry.

On their long journey out of Algonquin, logs had to be transported across numerous remote lakes. At one point in time, teams of workhorses, located on massive rafts, powered devices that pulled floating logs across lakes. Later, steam-powered tugs were used. These tugs, known as "alligators", could also winch themselves overland. Only three of these remarkable tugs are left in the world today. One of them, the "William M" pictured here, is on permanent display at the Logging Museum. Visitors can walk right into its boiler room.

The last few exhibits make use of video to recount the tension that grew between loggers and recreational users throughout the last half of the 1900's, the compromises reached between them, and the scope of present day logging in the Park. Modern day selective techniques employed by the Algonquin Forestry Authority are also presented.

The logging museum is also home to exciting events such as evening presentations given by Park staff dressed in costume as the ghosts of historical figures. In recent years, these Spirit Walks have been held on Mondays in July. Loggers' Day, held in late July, involves logging demonstrations and the telling of lumberjack stories. The uniqueness of this "trail" puts it in its own league. It is not included in the Trail Rankings Chart. You'll have to walk it yourself to see how it compares! The logging museum reception building is open daily from late May until mid-Oct; the walking trail is always open.

11

TOM THOMSON
Northern River, 1914 -1915
Oil on canvas
National Gallery of Canada, Ottawa

ART AND
ALGONQUIN PARK

Artists have long been drawn to the rugged beauty of Algonquin Park. On both a historical and a contemporary basis, the Park has come to hold a special place in the lives and the work of many of Canada's finest artists. Algonquin's splendors provided inspiration to the artists who banded together to form the Group of Seven, one of Canada's earliest and most important movements in Modern Art. In the green forests and cool waters of Algonquin Park, they found companionship, expression and solitude. Unfortunately, one of the country's most famous painters also found his death.

TOM THOMSON (1877 – 1917)

Tom Thomson is Canada's most legendary painter. He was able to capture the essence of landscape and crystallize a moment as effectively as any landscape artist in Canadian history. He was deeply moved by the natural world and by Algonquin Park specifically. For five brief but productive years preceding his tragic death in 1917, he dashed about the Park recording its many faces in his bold style of painting. His collection of oil works, which include lakeshores, sunsets, northern lights, lone pine trees, logging scenes and wild flowers has been described as a complete encyclopedia of Algonquin. His ability to summarize the moment with economy, and to interpret the scene in a way that is universally understood, was simply outstanding. Anyone standing in front of a Thomson painting shares the experience of the day it was painted and can perceive exactly how cold it was and what the wind was doing. Thomson never left anything in doubt about the quality of the day. He created some of the most recognized and influential Canadian paintings to date. He also played a key role in the growth of the Group of Seven, which is regarded as the first Canadian art movement to deal with the idea of wilderness in a non-European fashion. Today he is more popular than ever and his images are widely reproduced. His life as a woodsman and painter, and his suspicious death in the waters of an Algonquin Lake, continue to ignite the imaginations of the Canadian public.

His Beginnings

Tom grew up in the Province of Ontario on the shores of Georgian Bay. Childhood days in his small farming community were filled with outdoor adventures. Although he developed into a fine fisherman, he did not manage to finish high school, nor did he complete a machinist apprenticeship or courses in business. Natural lettering

TOM THOMSON
The West Wind, 1917
Oil on Canvas, 47.5 x 54 inches
Art Gallery of Ontario, Toronto
Gift of the Canadian Club of Toronto, 1926

The West Wind is one of the major icons of Canadian art.

skills eventually landed him employment in the commercial art industry in Toronto. As Tom approached his thirties, he began to place
more importance on painting. He left town frequently to take weekend sketching trips with other artists employed at the same firm. A
wealthy Toronto doctor who was impressed by Tom's sketches of
Algonquin Park provided encouragement and financial assistance
for Tom to leave his employment and to pursue his art more seriously. Tom developed a pattern of living and painting in Algonquin
Park from spring to late fall, and returning to Toronto each winter
to rework some of his smaller onsite works into larger studio paintings.

Canoes and Colour: Tom and the Park (1912-1917)

Tom made his own fishing lures, mastered the canoe, and spent as much time as possible on Algonquin Park's lakes and in its forests. His exploits as a woodsman were widely respected, even among professional guides. The story was often told of how he was once picking berries on one side of a log while a black bear was doing the same on the other! Tom supplemented his artist's income by taking casual work as a fishing guide or fire ranger.

Thomson's lifestyle was a perfect combination of his love for the outdoors and his passion for painting. He painted his own canoe with expensive artist oil paint in order to achieve the perfect combination of grey and blue. He paddled throughout the Park with his painting supplies, pausing frequently to capture the moment. On longer trips, he sometimes pushed off from shore on starry nights and slept on the bottom of his canoe as it drifted throughout the night and came to rest on a far shore in the morning.

He used oil on small 8 ½ x 10 inch boards of wood or cardboard. The small size allowed him to be portable. He painted on the spot, often in a furiously fast manner. Tales are told of Thomson dashing madly out into a storm to paint the sky, the clouds, or the water. When Thomson set out to paint a landscape, he attempted to capture the special quality or mood of the day, and his emotional response to it. When Thomson selected colours, he did not necessarily choose the ones which would result in a photographic reproduction of what lay in front of him, but rather the colours that nature suggested would work together to give the mood of the day.

His paintings were honest and direct interpretations of how he responded to what he saw. He translated his emotions into paint unhesitatingly in a manner which very few artists have been able to do. Many people looking at his paintings feel that they are communicating with nature, with the same clarity that nature communicated itself to him.

Tom was exceptionally critical of his work, occasionally flinging paintings into the trees in disgust, or scraping the oil paint off previously painted boards so that he could paint a new scene over them. He did not place much value on his paintings and would simply leave them in the bush if he had trouble carrying them all. He was also known to give them away to anyone expressing interest in them. He cared little for current theories of painting and even less about what the critics had to say of his work. His patron once commented on the fact that the only critics that Tom respected were the animals that chewed on his paintings when he left them out in the forest to dry.

The Long Winters In Toronto

Each winter Tom returned to Toronto to live among a circle of artist friends. His patron, who was also supporting other painters in this circle, had helped to build a specially designed studio building for them to live and work in. Tom, whose existence had become so in tune with nature, was uncomfortable within the confines of the Studio Building. Later, due to a lack of studio space, a small wooden shack located on the edges of the building's property, near a ravine, was renovated. Windows were added to capture the day's best painting light and Tom built himself a bunk-bed. In this shack he lived simply, and reworked his oil sketches into some of the most famous canvasses ever painted in Canada. He shied away from city life, painting throughout the day and sneaking out at night, when the city was asleep, to snowshoe through the wooded ravine.

Tom's Mysterious Death

A fellow artist by the name of Arthur Lismer said that Tom "never bragged of his painting but was mighty proud of his fishing". This pride led Tom to a running bet with a good friend and Park ranger regarding which of them would be the first to catch a particularly large trout which had managed to elude their hooks for sometime. Tom set out by himself in pursuit of that fish one clear summer day in 1917; he never returned. His upturned canoe was sighted adrift in Canoe Lake two days later. After an eight day search, his body was found floating in the waters of the same lake. The body had a large 4-inch bruise on the temple and a fishing line was wrapped 17 times around one of his ankles.

The inquest, which by some reports was held in a hasty and unprofessional manner, *after* the body was buried, proclaimed accidental drowning as the cause of death. Many area residents were immediately skeptical. Thomson's exploits on the water were well known. He was considered to be a strong enough swimmer to swim clear across Canoe Lake. In fact, Tom had aided Park rangers in the rescue of several boaters. Speculation as to the "real" circumstances of his death began to be heard almost immediately.

Opinions ranged from suicide to murder. Probably the most popular theory (supported strictly by circumstantial evidence) is that Tom encountered another canoeist on a portage trail between two lakes and that an argument between the two men escalated into a confrontation wherein Thomson was struck on the temple with a paddle blow that killed him. This popular theory asserts that the killer, likely surprised at the outcome of his actions and fearful of being discovered, dropped the body into the lake after weighing it down with a large rock attached by way of the fishing line found wrapped around its ankle. Proponents of this version of events point a finger at a man named Martin Bletcher, a heavy drinker who was known to possess a hot temper and who was reported to have had a crush on Winnie Trainor, who apparently was Tom's girlfriend. He had once warned Thomson to "stay out of my way if you know what is good for you". On the night before Tom's disappearance, the two men had a public disagreement so intense that they needed to be restrained in order to prevent them from coming to blows! Numerous attempts have been made to establish the true cause of death, but no one has been successful in convincing the authorities that foul play was involved.

A Memorial to Tom Thomson: the Cairn at Canoe Lake

A few months after his death, Tom's fellow artists and friends banded together to create a lasting tribute to him. A stone cairn was erected near Tom's favourite campsite at Hayhurst Point overlooking Canoe Lake. Its engraved bronze plate, designed by J.E.H. MacDonald reads:

To the memory of Tom Thomson, artist, woodsman and guide
who was drowned on Canoe Lake, July 8th 1917;
who lived humbly and passionately with the wild.
It made him the brother to all untamed things in nature.
It drew him apart and revealed itself wonderfully to him.
It sent him out from the woods only to show these revelations
through his art;
and it took him to itself at last.

Today the cairn maintains its watch from its perch high above the shoreline of Canoe Lake. Many Park visitors tie their canoes up at the wooden dock below it and scramble up the short, but steep path to the cairn and its commanding view over the blue waters of Canoe Lake. The adjacent totem pole, which guides canoeists in from Canoe Lake, was painted by camp counselors at the nearby Taylor Statton Camp and was erected in 1930.

Thomson and the Group of Seven

Several of the artists whom Tom worked with in the commercial art industry were also a part of life at the studio building in Toronto. They became some of Tom's closest friends. They shared the common vision of breaking away from the stuffy academic painting style of the times to express the Canadian identity in a new and original style. In many ways they pursued this goal as a collective. As they searched for a motif or theme with which to portray the Canadian spirit, their art found a heavy bias in wilderness and land. Tom Thomson was an integral part of this pursuit and he introduced his fellow artists to Algonquin Park and the "explorer" style of painting. Several made the trip to the Park to trudge across lakes with Thomson in canoes to reach painting spots. In its early days, this group loosely referred to itself as the Algonquin School.

Unfortunately, the collective was scattered by the First World War, and by the time they re-grouped in Toronto, Thomson was dead. In 1920, the remaining artists formalized their relationship and exhibited in Toronto under the name of the Group of Seven. The seven members were Franklin H. Carmichael, Lawren Harris, A.Y. Jackson, Frank H. Johnson, Arthur Lismer, J.E.H. MacDonald, and F.H. Varley. Their work caused controversy in Canadian art circles, but in a few years they were firmly established as a major force in Canadian Art. The group later invited other artists such as A.J. Casson, Edwin Holgate, and L.L.FitzGerald to join their movement. The Group of Seven remain immensely popular to this day; in fact, a Lawren Harris painting entitled *Lake Superior III* fetched roughly one million dollars at an art auction in 1999. This set a new record for the highest auction price ever paid in Canada for a Canadian painting. Some of the artists who painted in Algonquin Park have been honoured by having lakes named after them. If you look closely at the *Canoe Routes Map,* you'll see Tom Thomson Lake, Lismer Lake, Varley Lake and J.E.H. MacDonald Lake.

ROBERT BATEMAN
Great Blue Heron, 1978
acrylic, 30 x 40 inches

ROBERT BATEMAN (1930 -   )

Robert Bateman is one of the world's leading contemporary wild-life artists. He is an ecological painter interested in the relation-ships between habitat and wildlife. A respected naturalist, he stud-ies bird and mammals in depth and learns everything he possibly can about their lives. He often builds plasticene models prior to painting. Everything in his frames, from individual feathers to the geology and botany of landscape, is accurate. Although his works are seemingly detailed, he succeeds in capturing the illusion of re-ality through the use of light, shade and space. In 1981, he was commissioned to produce a loon painting to be given to Prince Charles and Lady Diana on behalf of the Government of Canada on the occasion of their wedding.

Bateman grew up in Toronto and at the ages of 17,18 and19, landed summer employment at a Government Wildlife Research Camp in Algonquin Park, later returning to the Park at the age of 21 to work at the Fisheries Research Lab on Opeongo Lake. Between washing dishes and disposing of garbage, he learned cataloguing and illustrative skills, how to catch and prepare specimens, complete a bird census and identify the call of the vast majority of the Park's birds. The budding artist respected Tom Thomson and the Group of Seven, and took every oppurtunity to load a canoe with paints and paddle off to places they had painted years before. Bateman recalls being pestered by persistent mosquitoes and black flies during these outings and claims that anyone looking closely at his works from that period will see several tiny insect bodies embedded in the oil paint!

Dwayne Harty (1957-)

Dwayne Harty's particular brand of genius arises out of his strong sense of colour, which he combines with draftsman skills and a thorough understanding of animals and their habitats. He creates wildlife portraits in a variety of mediums and he is well known for producing large background landscapes to which mounted animals and fabricated vegetation are added to create three-dimensional exhibits called dioramas. Harty's diorama work can be found in some of North America's finest museums including the Royal Ontario Museum in Toronto. In the early 1990's he was commissioned to design and execute five life-sized natural history dioramas for permanent display at the Algonquin Park Visitor Centre. Most of the work on this elaborate two-year project was done during the construction of the new building. When the building went without heat for a two-week period one winter, he simply donned a parka and continued painting!

Dwayne grew up in rural Saskatchewan and often accompanied his father on camping trips into the northern reaches of the prairie province. He became aware of the magic of Algonquin Park at an early age through the works of Tom Thomson. In his late teens and early twenties he studied with Clarence Tillenius at the Okanagan Summer School of the Arts, later benefiting from the tutelage of Robert Lougheed as he incorporated elements of such wildlife greats as Rungius, Kuhnert and Lijefors into his own style. He played a key role in bringing the prestigious Annual Exhibition of the Society of Animal Artists, the world's oldest association of animal and wildlife painters and sculptors, to Canada for the first time in 1995, when it was held in Algonquin Park.

DWAYNE HARTY
Otter
oil 12 x 16 inches

MAJOR GALLERIES:

The Algonquin Gallery, located in the Park (Hwy 60 at km 20), houses seasonal exhibits show-casing the work of well known Canadian landscape artists, such as Tom Thomson and the Group of Seven as well as many of the world's leading contemporary wildlife artists such as Robert Bateman and Dwayne Harty.   Its gift shop sells reproductions of works, books and other art-related products. A patio restaurant overlooks picturesque Found Lake.
(705) 788-1223, www.parkart.com

The McMichael Canadian Art Collection is located just 15 minutes east of Highway 400, the autoroute between Toronto and Algonquin Park. The 84,000 square foot gallery's collection of Tom Thomson and Group of Seven works is extensive and complimented by Thomson's old shack, which has been restored and relocated. Beautiful walking trails also lead visitors through the forested grounds. (905) 893-1211, www.mcmichael.on.ca

The National Gallery of Canada is located on the banks of the mighty Ottawa River, just minutes from the Parliament buildings in Canada's capital city of Ottawa. This 570,000 square foot gallery showcases the finest Canadian art, as well as masterpieces of the world's great artists. It is home to many Group of Seven pieces of art, and has the largest collection of Thomson works in the world. At time of writing, the gallery was implementing a powerful interactive package, which will allow online exploration of the Gallery. "CyberMuse" will allow users to not only view works from home, but also to access audio/video information about artists, pieces or art, and the stories behind them. Ottawa is roughly a four-hour drive from the Park's East Gate. 1-800-319-2787, http://national.gallery.ca

The Art Gallery of Ontario (AGO), located in downtown Toronto, is the eighth largest public gallery in North America. It was the site of the first Group of Seven exhibition and is home to many of their paintings, as well as some of Tom Thomson's most acclaimed pieces. The gallery's wonderful Canadian collection also includes numerous Inuit carvings. The Gallery lies three hours by car from the Park's West Gate. (416) 979-6648, www.ago.net

The Tom Thomson Memorial Gallery in Owen Sound was designed specifically to be a lasting tribute to the great artist. Its collection includes many of his works as well as Tom Thomson artifacts and numerous works by the Group of Seven. The Gallery website has extensive information on the life and works of Tom Thomson, as well as biographical sketches on each member of the Group of Seven. Owen Sound is located roughly 3.5 hours by car from Algonquin Park. (519) 376-1932, www.tomthomson.org

LOCAL GALLERIES

The Visitor Centre houses a small gallery located immediately to the left of its entrance. It is frequently home to exhibits of contemporary artists who work with an Algonquin Park theme.

The Madawaska Art Shop - two buildings of fine art including paintings, pottery, sculpture and glass. It is located approx 40 min from the East Gate. Take Highway 60 east, turn right at Hwy 127 and follow it to the shop at the end. (613) 338-2555

Artist Studios/Galleries

- *David Kay* paints Algonquin landscapes in oil, watercolour, ink and acrylic. His studio/gallery is located on the premises of the Algonquin East Gate Motel (5 km east of the East Gate on Hwy 60). (613) 637-2652
- *Jeff Miller*, an Algonquin landscape artist, maintains a Studio/ Gallery which is just off Hwy 60, roughly 12 km east of Huntsville: turn north onto Limberlost Road and then left almost immediately. (705) 635-2754, www.lookseepaint.com
- *Brenda Wainman-Goulet* creates bronze-onstone landscapes and whimsical figures. She was born in Algonquin Park; her father was Deputy Chief Ranger. Her studio is located just off Hwy 60, roughly 12 km east of Huntsville: turn north onto Limberlost Road, then left onto Upper Walker Lake Road and finally right at its stop sign. (705) 635-1996.
- *The Muskoka Autumn Studio Tour:* the region, bordering the Park to the South, is home to some of Canada's finest potters, painters and sculptors. Each fall, during a weekend in late September, they open their studios to the public, who have the unique oppurtunity to meet them, watch demonstrations and purchase work. Visitors provide their own transportation between the studios, which are marked on a brochure published yearly. The drive between studios amid the dazzling fall colours can be simply breathtaking. (705) 689-0660, www.muskoka.com/tour

Village of Wilno Galleries: The tiny hamlet of Wilno lies immediately east of Barry's Bay roughly 50 minutes from the Park's East Gate. It is home to a variety of artisans and crafts people whose work is showcased in several galleries and artist studios including:
- *The Wilno Craft Gallery* - Canadian crafts including blown glass (613) 756-3010.
- *Wilno Garden* gallery - paintings & pottery (613) 756-7890
- The *Wilno Station Gallery* - photography, paintings furniture and crafts by local artists (613) 756 9515.

Learn more about the history of Wilno and its artisans at: www.wilno.com

Further Interest

- The Visitor Centre houses a Tom Thomson display that includes 10 reproductions of his oils, a replica of the memorial cairn and a life-size bust.
- Jeff Miller has created a nature/art/watercolour learning program for children and adults. He produces a video/art kit entitled Look See Paint and often conducts summer workshops in the Park
- The potential for an Academy of Wilderness and Wildlife Art based in the Algonquin Park is currently being assessed. Contact Wildlife Art Int. for more details (705)788-1223
- A comprehensive art supply shop is located in Huntsville: North Art Supplies (705)788-0726
- See the *Day Trip #1* chapter of this book for a map which can lead you to historical sites related to Tom Thomson.
- Addison, Ottelyn. Tom Thomson: the Algonquin Years. McGraw-Hill Ryerson Limited. 1975
- Four hard cover "coffee table" books showcase the art of Robert Bateman. The latest one is entitled *Robert Bateman: Natural Worlds* (Penguin/Madison Press, Toronto, 1996.)
- Robert Bateman's philosophical writings on the environment, education and other topics can be visited at www.batemanideas.com

12

LEARNING
SAFE CANOE
OPERATION

Among the world's premiere canoeing destinations, Algonquin Park is at its finest when seen from a canoe. Although the basics of safe canoe operation can be learned in a day, the boat's tipsy nature can lead to potentially dangerous, even tragic, situations for those who do not take the time to properly learn the basics. Learning directly from an experienced canoeist is the best option. Many opportunities are available to Park visitors both before they arrive and while they are in the Park.

Canoe Courses

1) The Ontario Recreational Canoe Association (ORCA) offers free one-day safe-canoeing courses in the Park at various times throughout the summer. In the morning, instructors demonstrate techniques which participants practice in the afternoon. Participants can bring their own equipment or share the canoes and paddles that are provided. No advance registration is required.*

2) Algonquin Outfitters, The Portage Store, Opeongo Algonquin, and Bartlett Lodge offer one-day guided trips in which participants are shown the basics and then taken on a paddling adventure. Sessions run between five and seven days a week, depending on the time of year. All equipment is provided. Call ahead to reserve.*

3) Instructional sessions are sometimes offered by Park Staff in the summer to those able to bring their own equipment.*

* Consult campground bulletin boards, Park Outfitters or Park staff for details.

A Photographic Canoe Manual for $1.00!!!!!

A $1.00 booklet entitled *The Canoeist's Manual* by Omer Stringer depicts, with the help of great instructional photos, safe exit/entry, lifting the canoe to your shoulders for portaging, steering with the J-stroke and solo canoeing. You can find this handy manual at the Visitor Centre and at area Outfitters.

Other recommended instruction books include:
* *The Path of the Paddle: An Illustrated Guide to the Art of Canoeing* by Bill Mason. (Key Porter Books, Toronto, 1984).
* *Cradle to Canoe – Camping and Canoeing with Children* by Rolf and Debra Kraiker. (Boston Mills Press, 1999).

A Few of the Most Important Rules and Procedures

The following recommendations apply to a canoe operated by two people. They do not, in themselves, constitute all that one should know about safe canoe operation. For safety reasons, it is best to learn directly from an instructor and to practice with an experienced canoeist.

1) Each occupant should wear a Personal Flotation Device (PFD) at all times. It is illegal to depart without them. Each canoe must, by law, also be equipped with a whistle, floating rope (15 m), a water-tight flashlight and a bailer.

2) Both canoeists face the front of the boat. The front is the end with the greater distance between the seat and the tip of the canoe.

3) The more skilled canoeist occupies the back and is responsible for steering with a rudder-like action of the paddle known as the J-stroke.

4) One hand is placed on top of the paddle while the other grasps the shaft close to the blade; partners paddle in rhythm, on opposite sides of the canoe. Paddlers switch sides occasionally, doing so at the same time to promote stability.

5) Mishaps often occur while entering into, or exiting from the canoe - ask an outfitter/staff member for a demonstration of proper technique.

6) Keep weight as close to the floor as possible. Kneeling on the canoe's floor, while resting one's "bum" on the seat, provides the most stability. Sitting directly on the seat generally is acceptable for calm conditions. NEVER stand up in a canoe.

7) Gear of substantial weight should be placed in the middle of the canoe on the floor. Do not tie heavy backpacks, etc. to the canoe.

8) Always try to paddle close to shore. Turn the craft directly into the path of larger waves.

9) Avoid canoeing in the dark, high winds, overly rough water or other adverse weather conditions. Do not canoe in electrical storms.

10) On land, canoes are designed to be carried upside down on the canoeist's shoulders. Ask an outfitter/staff member for a demonstration.

Wayne Van Sickle

Portaging a canoe

Further Interest:
- CRCA – (Canadian Recreational Canoeing Association): offers certification courses; produces several free publications including a safe canoeing booklet and a catalogue of over 1000 canoe and kayak books, maps, videos, etc.; publishes Kanawa, a subscription canoeing and kayaking magazine; organizes The Waterwalker Film Festival. Headquartered at Ron Johnstone Paddling Centre on Rideau River in Merrickville, Ontario, (613) 269-2910, www.crca.ca.
- ORCA – (Ontario Recreational Canoeing Association): produces free "how-to" brochures; offers canoeing and kayaking certification courses. Contact ORCA through Canoe Ontario.
- Canoe Ontario – an umbrella association for several Ontario canoe organizations: sells books, videos and maps, produces quarterly Canoeing Ontario magazine, (416) 426-7170, www.canoeontario.on.ca.
- The Canadian Canoe Museum in Peterborough, Ontario: the world's largest collection of canoes (early birch bark to modern day). Preserves vessels and recounts the stories of the canoe. Courses in traditional canoe and paddle building. Helps organize the Annual Heritage Canoe Festival held in early May, (705) 748-9153, www.canoemuseum.net.
- Canoe Expo – the largest canoe and kayak exhibition in Canada. Takes place annually in March at the Metro East Trade Centre in Pickering Ontario, (416) 426-7170, www.canoeontario.on.ca.

DAY TRIP # 1

CANOE LAKE

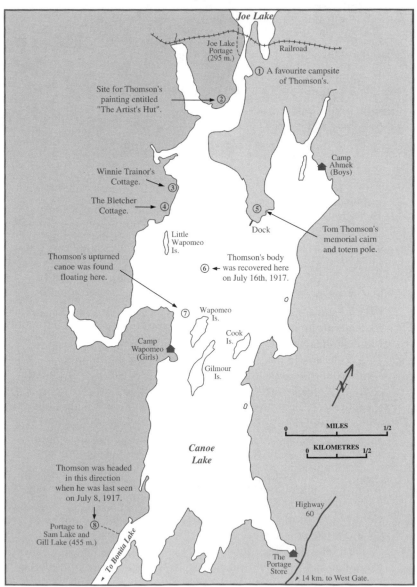

Joe Lake

Joe Lake Portage (295 m.)

Railroad

① A favourite campsite of Thomson's.

Site for Thomson's painting entitled "The Artist's Hut". ②

Camp Ahmek (Boys)

Winnie Trainor's Cottage. ③

The Bletcher Cottage. ④

⑤

Dock

Tom Thomson's memorial cairn and totem pole.

Little Wapomeo Is.

Thomson's body ⑥ ← was recovered here on July 16th, 1917.

Thomson's upturned canoe was found floating here.

⑦ Wapomeo Is.

Camp Wapomeo (Girls)

Cook Is.

Gilmour Is.

Canoe Lake

MILES
0 ———— 1/2

KILOMETRES
0 ———— 1/2

Highway 60

Thomson was headed in this direction when he was last seen on July 8, 1917.

Portage to Sam Lake and Gill Lake (455 m.) ⑧

To Bonita Lake

The Portage Store

14 km. to West Gate.

Themes: Canoeing – Lakes – Park History -Tom Thomson – Portaging a Canoe – Restaurant, Gift Shop

Canoe Lake, which is about 4 km long from tip to tip, has been the centre of much activity over the years. In fact, it is arguably the most richly historical lake in the Park. It was named in 1853 by a geological survey team which stopped along its shores to build a canoe. In the early 1900's, Canoe Lake Station was a busy stop along the logging railroad, which also brought the first tourists to Algonquin Park. Throughout the years many people have been impressed with the beauty of Canoe Lake. Foremost among them was Tom Thomson - the legendary Canadian landscape artist and outdoorsman. The rugged lakeshore provided many of his favourite sketching locations and campsites. A bronze and stone cairn, over-looking Canoe Lake, was erected in his memory shortly after he drowned mysteriously in its waters in 1917. Today Canoe Lake is the most popular access point for those embarking on multi-day canoe trips in the Park's Interior. Its historic character and scenic quality combine with its onsite canoe rental service, restaurant, ice cream stand and large gift shop, to make it a great location for day trips ranging from a few hours to the better part of the day.

Canoe Rentals

The Portage Store, located directly on the lake, rents canoes for full or half days, in addition to providing comprehensive outfitting services to those embarking on multi-day trips. Demand can be heavy (especially on weekends in July and August) and visitors are best advised to make a reservation a day or two in advance. It is important to size up the weather conditions on Canoe Lake and communicate your experience level to the rental staff upon arrival. One day can make a world of difference in Algonquin Park and rather than braving high winds, waves or other hazards, it may be wise to simply return the following day. The *Learning Safe Canoe Operation* chapter contains information about how to learn canoe skills. Rental staff can provide a quick onsite demonstration of portaging technique and the J-stroke.

Tom Thomson Sites

You'll find an overview of the life and times of Tom Thomson in the chapter entitled *Art and Algonquin*. One of the most enjoyable ways to explore the lake and its personable shoreline is to read that chapter and then use the *Canoe Lake Map* to navigate between the various Tom Thomson sites. The view from the Tom Thomson Cairn is spectacular. Many visitors tie up their canoe at the public dock below, and scramble up the short but steep path to the monument. The one-way paddle between the cairn and the Portage Store generally takes between 45 minutes and one hour, depending on the skill level of the canoeists and the strength and direction of the prevailing wind.

Joe Lake Portage

A 295 m footpath leading to Joe Lake is found at the extreme northwest tip of the lake. Many of Algonquin's lakes are not linked by navigable waterways, and adventurers on multi-day canoe trips carry their vessel and all of their camping gear along trails like this (otherwise known as "portages") every day. Day-trippers wanting to explore Joe Lake, or simply wanting to add portaging skills to their repertoire, should hoist their canoe upside down onto their shoulders and march off down the trail. Those wishing to simply walk to Joe Lake and appreciate the scenery should ensure that their canoe is pulled well up and off to the side of the landing, so as not to hold up multi-day trippers who might need to unload at the portage. A word to the wise – canoes made of different materials vary greatly in terms of weight. Anyone wishing to try his or her hand at portaging will likely appreciate a lightweight vessel constructed from kevlar.

Notes and Optional Preparatory Reading:

- *The Canoeist Manual** by Omar Stringer ($1.00) has great instructional photos demonstrating the art of lifting a canoe to your shoulders for portaging.
- *Canoe Lake, Algonquin Park: Tom Thomson and Other Mysteries* by S. Bernard Shaw, sheds additional light on Canoe Lake's shady past.
- Topographical precision is found on the *Canoe Lake Day-Tripper Map* by Chrismar Mapping - an excellent, waterproof map.
- Canoe Lake's cottages, including those marked on the map, are private property; please respect people's privacy.
- Camp Wapomeo and Camp Ahmek can be visited on the web at www.camp.ca/tsc/.

DAYTRIP # 2

OPEONGO LAKE & COSTELLO CREEK

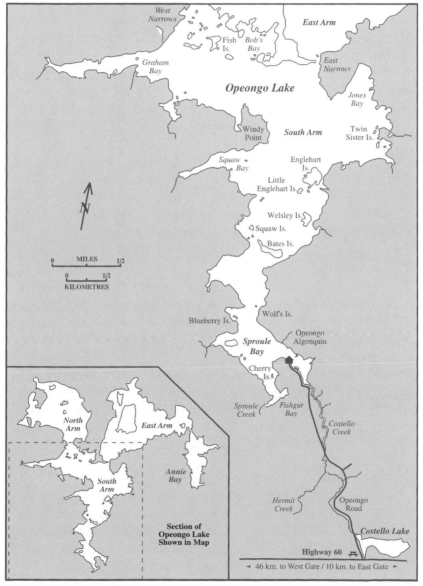

West Narrows

East Arm

Fish Is.

Bob's Bay

Graham Bay

East Narrows

Opeongo Lake

Jones Bay

Windy Point

South Arm

Twin Sister Is.

Squaw Bay

Englehart Is.

Little Englehart Is.

Welsley Is.

Squaw Is.

Bates Is.

N

0 MILES 1/2

0 1/2
KILOMETRES

Wolf's Is.

Blueberry Is.

Opeongo Algonquin

Sproule Bay

Cherry Is.

Sproule Creek

Fishgut Bay

Costello Creek

North Arm

East Arm

Annie Bay

South Arm

Hermit Creek

Opeongo Road

Section of
Opeongo Lake
Shown in Map

Costello Lake

Highway 60

◄ 46 km. to West Gate / 10 km. to East Gate ►

Themes: Canoeing - Creeks - Algonquin's Largest Lake - Wildlife Encounters,

Algonquin's cozy creeks and streams offer a very different canoeing experience than its grand lakes. Travel on a large lake provides an opportunity for visitors to appreciate the scale of the Park. The canoe in which they float is but a tiny dot on the wide-open expanse of a great Algonquin lake. The experience of sitting or kneeling in a canoe close to the waves, and feeling the wind rush up on you from the far side of the lake, is a perfect demonstration of the reason Canada is known for its wide-open spaces. Travelling down a narrow meandering creek is a different story altogether. Visitors become an integral part of the surroundings. Plants reach out and touch the canoe; paddles occasionally dig into the muddy bottom. The sources of noises are more easily located and canoeists find themselves close to anything that moves.

The Opeongo Day-Tripping Area provides visitors with a chance to partake in both of these canoeing experiences and does so with flair. Opeongo Lake is by far the biggest lake in Algonquin Park; Costello Creek has a well-earned reputation for being one of the Park's most reliable and scenic places to encounter wildlife.

Canoe Rentals

Canoes can be rented at the Opeongo Algonquin Store. The store is located directly at the water's edge, where the southern terminus of Opeongo Lake meets the mouth of Costello Creek. Day-trippers starting out from the outfitter's dock can paddle up-country into the great expanse of Opeongo Lake or down into the calm waters of Costello Creek; many take the time to do both. Opeongo Algonquin is reached via a 6 km road leading north from Highway 60 at km 46.3. The store provides comprehensive outfitting services to those setting out on multi-day trips, and also has T-shirts, books and edibles. It is wise to call ahead to reserve a canoe.

Opeongo Lake

"Opeongo" is derived from a Native American word meaning "lake that is sandy at the narrows". Canoeists will indeed see sandbars along Algonquin's characteristically rugged and rocky shoreline. When I think of Opeongo Lake, I think of great swimming and fabulous sunsets. In fact, the silhouetted images displayed on the covers of both of my Algonquin Park books were taken at this Lake. On a calm, clear day, "Opeongo" can be as much fun to paddle, as it is to pronounce. Its twisted shoreline and numerous small islands are a canoeist's delight. It can also be a rewarding area for birdwatchers. The outfitting store's staff generally locates over 30 nesting pairs of loons on the lake each year. Canoeists also have some of the best oppurtunities to spot birds such as the Merlin (*Falco columbarius*) and the Osprey (*Pandion haliaetus*) which are uncommon in Algonquin Park. Merlins (small falcons capable of speeds greater than 80 km/h) have traditionally nested in the islands at the top of the lake's southern arm, and in the area between the Opeongo Algonquin Store and Cherry Island. The lake also has a well-earned reputation among anglers. Lake and Brook trout are most commonly caught in the spring, while visitors armed with nothing more than a hook, a worm and a bobber can reel in Bass in July and August. Depending on skill level, paddlers can expect to make the journey between the Opeongo Algonquin Store and Bates Island in one to two hours. Algonquin's lakes are best enjoyed on calm, clear days. This is particularly true in the case of Opeongo Lake, which produces some of the Park's largest and most dangerous waves on bad weather days. I recommend that you make rental staff aware of your skill level upon arrival. If conditions on the lake overwhelm your abilities, staff may recommend that you stick to the creek or come back a day later. Information about how to learn to canoe can be found in the chapter entitled *Learning Safe Canoe Operation*.

Costello Creek:

Costello Creek is a picturesque stream, winding through low-lying territory that is rich in wildlife. Impressive cliffs rise to the east. The Creek is quite calm and easily negotiated in either direction. In the summertime, moose are sometimes spotted up to their eyeballs in the creek feasting on large Yellow Water-lilies. Otters and beavers frequent the waterway, Great Blue Herons stand at its edge and Gray Jays reside in the nearby forest. A leisurely paddle down the creek is splendid at any time of the day, but those particularly interested in its wildlife should plan to visit around dawn or dusk when animal activity is at its highest. The creek becomes largely impassable after it meets Opeongo Road (see map); most people turn around at that point and return to the lake. A leisurely paddle from the outfitter's dock to the road takes about one hour, one way.

Notes and Optional Preparatory Reading:

- Depending on the time of year, the outfitter may open after dawn or close before dusk (call to confirm times). Those wishing to paddle a rental canoe outside of their operating hours, should make special arrangements with the outfitter well in advance.
- *Lake Opeongo: Untold Stories of Algonquin Park's Largest Lake* by S. Bernard Shaw is an account of some of the many strange and historical events that have occurred in and around the Lake during the last 150 years.
- Each and every angle of shoreline has been painstakingly mapped on the topographical and waterproof *Opeongo Lake Day-Tripper Map* by Chrismar Mapping.

14

Wayne Van Sickle

PLANNING AN
INTERIOR TRIP

The Interior of the Park refers to regions accessible strictly by canoe or by foot. Interior travelers camp at designated sites, along lakes or rivers, which accommodate one party of up to 9 persons. A number of regulations govern Interior travel and routes must be registered prior to departure. Heavy demand makes it imperative to reserve routes as far in advance as possible, and to contact an outfitter in the initial planning stages should canoe or equipment rentals, or other outfitting services, be required. Embarking on a journey into the unpopulated regions of Algonquin Park is not a trivial matter. The demands of self-sufficiency and the possibility of adverse weather conditions can lead to dangerous, if not tragic, situations. There is no substitute for experience in the backcountry. Those without it should hire a guide or consider joining an experienced group.

Time of year considerations
Canoeing season begins in early May, despite dangerously cold waters. Water temperatures warm sufficiently for most canoeists by June and remain acceptable until mid-October. August and September, which are comparatively bug-free, are the best times.
Prime backpacking season runs from early August to late October. Trips in May trips can be incredible, but difficult to plan in advance due to somewhat unpredictable temperatures. Biting insects are almost unbearable from late May through early July. Trips planned for later than October risk cold weather.

Route planning and registration
Canoe trippers and hikers must register a detailed trip itinerary at time of reservation. Itineraries include the access points from which the trip will commence and conclude, and the sites of each proposed camp. The *Canoe Routes of Algonquin Provincial Park Map* and *Backpacking Trails of Algonquin Provincial Park M*ap show the locations of campsites and access points. The backsides are printed with information regarding rules, regulations, fees, gear requirements, food selection, reserving the route as well as locations and contact numbers for outfitters. Acquiring one of these maps is the first step. They are carried by most outfitters in Ontario, and are distributed worldwide by The Friends of Algonquin Park (email: orders@algonquinpark.on.ca, tel: (613) 637-2828). The portion of the map that shows campsites, lakes and portages can be downloaded for free at www.ontarioparks.com/algpdf.html.

- **Canoe trips**

Algonquin Park does not have defined canoe routes, but rather one vast, interconnected network of 29 access points, 1400 campsites and numerous portage trails from which an almost limitless number of routes can be designed. Planning a route becomes relatively simple after an access point is chosen. The largest numbers of trippers start from one of the 9 access points (#'s 5 to13) located along Highway 60. They are easy to get to and close to Park facilities and outfitters. They are also very busy. Access Points #5 and #11 have great onsite outfitting services. Remote access points are quieter and much less travelled. Many have an outfitter located nearby. The trade-off with remote access points is that users can experience greater travel time from home to lake, a loss in proximity to other facilities and generally less convenience (convenience and remoteness are never found together). Some outfitters will transport canoes and rented items to access points.

After choosing the access point, the next step is to pick the lakes where you will camp each night. Most canoeists travel between 15 and 25 km each day (including portages). A string cut to represent the length of daily travel (use the map's scale) helps to determine the lakes within each day's range. Pick one at the low end of the range for the first night. Although most lakes have more than one campsite, the Reservation System does not distinguish between particular sites (for example, the lake's most northern or most southern site). The service issues nightly reservations for each lake until the number of reservations equals the number of sites on that lake.

Additional tips:

1) "Portages" are land trails that connect lakes not linked by navigable water. They are a daily part of most trips. Creativity at the planning stage can minimize their number and length.

2) Most trippers incorporate at least one non-travelling day into their route for relaxation and exploration.

3) Trips beginning and ending at the same Access Point simplify logistics.

Kevin Callan's book, *Brook Trout and Blackflies: a Paddler's Guide to Algonquin Park*, (Boston Mills Press) provides detailed information on many of his favourite routes.

Wayne Van Sickle

These campers are baking "bannock" - a modern day version of traditional Native American bread. A recipe is listed in the further interest section.

- **Backpacking**

The planning process is similar to that of canoe trips, but simpler due to the existence of established trails. There are two access points along Highway 60 and two remote ones. Once the access point has been selected, the next step is to choose campsites for each night. Backpackers generally cover between 8 – 15 km a day.

Food choices

The necessary Park maps provide menu suggestions, so I won't go into too much detail, except to offer some easy vegetarian options. There is a total ban on bottles and cans in the Park Interior; most visitors make use of "ziplock" bags and plastic cannisters.

Breakfast: Bannock. Hot cereals such as instant oatmeal packets, cream of wheat, rice porridge or cornmeal topped with dried berries, almond flakes, sunflower seeds, sugar or cinnamon.

Lunch: Hard rye bread crackers with dried mixes such as hummus, black bean, tabbouleh, refried beans. Peanut butter and jam sandwiches. Soup mixes and bannock. Bagels, cream cheese and vegetables will stay fresh for the first few days.

Dinner: Dinners can be based on couscous, pasta, basmati rice or vegetarian chili mix. Sauces can be made from pesto or tomato soup mix packets. Dinners can be fine-tuned with dehydrated

vegetable flakes and spices. Lipton instant noodle packages.
A wide variety of individual freeze dried meals can be purchased at
local outfitting stores. Some outfitters also offer custom food packs
consisting of enough ready to cook meals for the entire trip.

Further Interest
- A life-size Interior campsite exhibit, complete with a properly loaded canoe, hanging bear-proof pack and necessary equipment is on display at the Canoe Lake Permit Office.
- O.R.C.A. sells instructional books on canoe tripping, conducts tripping courses and produces a free series of canoe trip how-to brochures (equipment list, food and menu, first aid kit, planning), (416) 426-7170, www.canoeontario.on.ca.
- *The Complete Canoe Trip Planner* by Gignac, W & Rudolph, J. (Magnetic North Wilderness Adventures, Ancaster, 1998) helps trippers through the necessary planning steps.
- *Chrismar Mapping Algonquin Park Map Series* – waterproof, topographical maps (1:80,000-scale) with Interior campsites and portages.
- The Canada Map Office produces a series of 17 topographical (1:50,000-scale) maps that completely cover the Park.
- An Interior Tabloid Newspaper containing "easy camping tips", regulations, menu ideas and other information is available at Park Gates.
- A bannock recipe for six:

At home combine and pack in a ziplock bag or plastic cannister:
340 ml. (1 1/2 cups) white flour • 340 ml. (1 1/2 cups) whole wheat flour • 42.5 ml (3 tbsp.) baking powder • 75 ml. (1/3 cup) skim milk powder • 5 ml. (1 tsp.) white sugar • a pinch of salt.

In camp:
-place mix in a pot, add 225 ml. (1 cup) water and knead till breadlike.
-form round 1/2 inch thick "patties".
-place a patty in a little oil in a heated pan, cover with lid or tin foil.
-bake each side for 7-10 minutes on low heat or until each side is brown

Some campers bake a large batch for breakfast and pack the leftovers for lunch. Bannock can be eaten plain or with honey or jam. For variety include berries, raisons, M&M's, nuts etc in the mix. Apple cinnamon bannock can be made with rehydrated dried apples and cinnamon spice. My favourite variety is topped with raspberry jam and brie cheese.

15

INFORMATION

Park Information Office
Information about all aspects of Algonquin Park can be obtained by telephone at (705) 633-5572 or by visiting the Park's website at www.algonquinpark.on.ca. While visiting the Park, information is best obtained in person at the Visitor Centre or at the East or West Gate.

The Reservation Service
Algonquin's campsites (interior and campground), cabins and yurts can be reserved by calling 1-888-668-7275. (Overseas callers may need to place their call with a Canadian operator). The service is available 24 hours a day, 7 days a week and accepts payment by Visa or Mastercard. Reservations are accepted up to 11 months in advance. The service handles all of Ontario's Provincial Parks and is for reservations only. Any questions specific to your route or Algonquin Park should be directed to the Algonquin Park Information Office before contacting the reservation service. Reservations may also be made at www.ontarioparks.com. The Website also contains basic information about all of Ontario's Provincial Parks.

Tourism Ontario
General information about travelling in Ontario, including attractions and lodging, as well as phone numbers for the tourist boards of other Canadian Provinces can be obtained by calling 1-800-668-2746 or (416) 203-2500 or by visiting www.travelinx.com.

Resorts Ontario
Information regarding several resorts, country inns, house-keeping resorts, and fishing lodges is available by calling 1-800-363-7227 or (705) 325-9115 or by visiting their web sites at www.resorts-ontario.com.

16

Wayne Van Sickle

SERVICES AND FACILITIES

Over 400, 000 people visit Algonquin Park each year. A well developed system of services and facilites exists in and around the Park. There are numerous options for accomodation, dining and outfitting. There are also several first-class learning and cultural facilties. Algonquin Park has four developed regions that are accessible by automobile; the Highway 60 Corridor, the East Side, the North Side and Algonquin South. The Highway 60 Corridor area of the Park is by far the most developed region. Each of the four areas has its own unique appeal.

A typical Algonquin Park Interior campsite.

Accommodation within the Park: all options are in heavy demand; book as far ahead as possible.

• *Interior Campsites:*
There are over 1500 campsites, which consist of a fire pit, a pit toilet and a tent clearing. These sites are reachable only by canoe or by foot.

• *Campgrounds:*
There are eight campgrounds situated in the Parkway Corridor. Some have showers, laundry facilities, electricity and RV hook-ups, while others are more basic. Sites are available for persons with physical handicaps. Mew Lake Campground remains open year round , while the others are seasonal. Consult with the Algonquin Park Information Service or the Park website for assistance in choosing the one most closely matched to your needs. Campgrounds are also located in Algonquin South, the Park's East Side and the Park's North Side.

• *Interior Cabins:*
A limited number of historic Ranger Cabins in the Park's Interior have been converted for public use and may be rented out on a nightly basis by one party at a time. In most instances, they are reachable only by canoe or by foot. Call the Park Information Office for a pamphlet with details.

Wayne Van Sickle

The Kitty Lake Cabin is one of the largest Ranger Cabins available for rent. It is located roughly one hour by canoe from Access Point # 17. The Old Ranger Cabin Rental Program was initiated in 1998 with the restoration of 12 cabins. Park administrators plan to add gradually to this number.

- *Canvas-roofed Shelters:*

Canvas-roofed shelters are available year round at the Mew Lake Campground (km 30.5). They sleep up to six people and are approximately five metres in diameter. Each has an electric heater, flourescent lighting, a propane barbeque, bunk beds, chairs, and a table. Kitchen utensils are provided during the summer months.

- *First Class Lodges Within the Park:*

Three lodges within the Park provide first class accommodation and fine dining from late May until mid-October. Generally guests are treated to two or three meals per day, as well as the use of lodge facilities, which can include canoes, saunas and tennis courts. Rates vary with the season. Reservations are highly recommended; contact the lodges directly:

Arowhon Pines Lodge: 705 633-5661   www.arowhonpines.ca
Bartlett Lodge: 705 633-5543   www.bartlettlodge.com
Killarney Lodge: 705 633-5551   www.killarneylodge.com

Lodges, Resorts, Inns & Motels Located Outside of The Park:

Whitney, Ontario
Algonquin Bed and Breakfast: 613 637-2847
Algonquin East Gate Motel: 613 637-2652   www.mv.igs.net/outfitters
Algonquin Parkway Inn: 613 637-2760   alpkinn@bancom.net
Bear Trail Inn Couples Resort: 613 637-2662   www.beartrailresort.com
Hay Lake Lodge: 613 637-2675   haylake@mv.igs.net
Riverview Cottages: 613 637-2690   www.riverviewcottages.com

Dwight, Ontario
Algonquin Lakeside Inn: 705 635-2434   www.travelinx.com
Blue Spruce Inn: 705 635-2330   www.travelinx.com
Bondi Village Resort: 705 635-2261   www.bondi-cottage-resort.com
Clover Leaf Cottages: 705 635-2049
Curv-Inn: 705 635-1892
Dwight Village Motel: 705 635-2400
Glen Manor Cottages: 705 635-1528   www.travelinx.com
Lakewoods 4 Season Resort: 705 635-2087   www.lakewoodsresort.com
Logging Chain Lodge: 705 635-2575   www.loggingchainlodge.on.ca
Lumina Resort: 705 635-2991   www.luminaresort.com
Nor Loch Lodge and Resort: 705 635-2231
Oxtongue Lake Cottages: 705 635-2951
Parkway Cottage Resort: 705 635-2763   www.travelinx.com
Port Cunnington Lodge: 705 635-2505   www.pc-lodge.com
Riverside Motel: 705 635-1677
Spring Lake Resort: 705 635-1562   www.springlakeresort.on.ca
Timber Trail Algonquin: 705 635-1097   www.timbertrail-algonquin.on.c&
White Birches Resort: 705 635-2322   www.travelinx.com

Restaurants in the Park:
- Each of the three lodges located in the Park offers outstanding multi-course meals to the public. Reservations are required. The lodges are not licensed to sell alcoholic beverages. Guests may bring their own wine and servers will uncork the bottle.
- The Portage Store Restaurant (km 14) overlooking historic Canoe Lake, serves full course meals, beer and wine.
- The Lake of Two Rivers Store (km 31.5) offers fast food items such as hamburgers and french fries, as well as ice cream.
- The Gallery Café at the Algonquin Gallery (km 20) serves interesting gourmet-like selections on an outdoor deck above picturesque Found Lake. Plans are in the works to sell beer and wine.

- The Sunday Creek Café at the Visitor Centre (km 43) offers lasagne, french-fries, pastries and a wide range of cafeteria food, including a salad and fruit bar.

Alcoholic Beverages in the Park:

Strict rules govern the consumption of alcoholic beverages; infractions may result in ejection from the Park and difficulties with the police. Consumption is prohibited at Park picnic areas, beaches, trails, parking lots, etc. Within the campgrounds, it may be consumed only at your campsite. Beer, wine and liquor are not available for sale in the Park. The nearest retail outlets are in the towns of Whitney (5 km east of the Park on Highway 60) and Huntsville (43 km west of the Park on Highway 60). When transporting alcohol via automobiles in the Province of Ontario, the law requires that it be kept in a place "not readily accessible to the driver". The best idea is to keep it in the trunk.

Equipment Sales/Rentals and Guides:

Virtually anything used to enjoy Algonquin Park's outdoors can be rented or purchased locally. See the *Outfitting Chart* located near the back of the book for details of who provides what.

Gasoline:

Gasoline is available at the Portage Store at km 14. Prices are high compared to those at the gas stations found along Highway 60 on either side of the Park.

Transportation to and from Toronto:

Canadian Woodlands Shuttle Service (416-515-0592, cdnwood@interlog.com) runs between Toronto and Algonquin Park, three to four times a week between late May and mid-October. Special runs, including those to and from Toronto International Airport, can be arranged for groups. Other bus lines connect Toronto and nearby towns; however, Canadian Woodlands is the only one to take passengers directly into the Park. Spaces fill quickly and reservations are required. The Shuttle accepts cash or travellers cheques only. No such service is available as of yet between the Park and Ottawa.

The Visitor Centre is a world- class faciltiy.

Gift and Book Stores in the Park:

- Visitor Centre at km 43: a gift shop with the largest selection of books in the Park. Profits are used to expand the range of Algonquin's Interpretive and Educational Products and Services.
- The Logging Museum: a history oriented bookstore and gift shop.
- The Portage Store (km 14) has a very large gift store which also sells books.
- The Two River's Store (km 31.5) has a small grocery store, and also sells film, souvenirs and postcards.
- Opeongo Algonquin Store, on Opeongo Road, specializes in products required for canoe tripping and also has meat, fruit, sandwiches, camping gear and souvenirs.

Museums

- The Visitor Centre (km 43) is a world-class facility. Historians, naturalists and artists have crafted over 25 exhibits to teach visitors about the Park's natural and human history. There are several true-to-life recreations of Park settings, complete with mounted animals such moose, wolves, bears, deer, beavers, loons and owls. A short film entitled *Images of Algonquin* runs

The observation deck at the Visitor Centre offers an expansive and spectacular view.

continuously in a large comfortable theatre, while special art and science exhibits are housed in a small gallery just inside the doors. There is also a book and gift shop and a cafeteria. The Centre's large walkout observation deck overlooks a mixed forest, a stream and two lakes. The Visitor Centre is open daily from late April to the end of October and weekends thereafter. It is also open daily during the Christmas holidays, Spring Break and Easter.

- The Logging Museum, located at km 54.6, contains displays and exhibits regarding the history and practice of logging in the Park. Most exhibits are located along an outdoor trail. See the *Logging Museum Trail* section for more details.
- The Algonquin Gallery, located at km 20, provides visitors with the oppurtuntiy to view paintings by Canadian landscape legends such as Tom Thomson and the Group of Seven, as well as works by many of the world's leading contemporary wildlife artists. See the *Art and Algonquin Park* chapter of this book for details.

Algonquin South

Algonquin South refers to the area accessible by way of Access Point # 15 – Kingscote Lake. The access point lies 58 km north-east of Haliburton and 52 km north-west of Bancroft. Its facilities and activities include:

- Campsites - There is a cluster of campsites located at the access point on Kingscote Lake. There are vault toilets but no showers or laundry facilities.
- Interior Routes - A variety of small lakes provide opportunities for one to three day canoe trips.
- High Falls Hiking Trail - A 1.9 km trail that follows an old road through a red pine plantation before turning into a footpath travelling through a hardwood forest. It leads to a great view of the rapids upstream of High Falls on the York River.
- Byers Lake Mountain Biking Trail - A 5 km trail, which follows an old logging road from the High Falls Parking Area to Byers Lake.
- Cross Country Skiing: Algonquin Nordic Wilderness Lodge grooms 80 km of trails. The lodge is located on a secluded lake on the edge of the Park. It provides meals, hot tubs, saunas and ski/snowshoe clinics. Guests must ski in 2.7 km from its parking lot. (705) 745-9497
- Horseback Riding: Over 50 km of spectacular trails are available on a day trip basis. Overnight rides are being considered for the future. Equestrian Outfitting Services are provided by South Algonquin Trails, who also offer guided trail rides for those without their own horses and parking for trailers in its lot, located across from the High Falls Parking Area. 1-800-758-4801 www.southalgonquintrails.com
- Interior Day Hiking Trails (not reachable by car): The Scorch Lake Lookout Trail and the Bruton Farm Hiking Trail start from the shores of Scorch Lake - a full day canoe journey from Access Point # 15. Scorch Lake Lookout Trail rises very steeply through a hardwood forest and culminates in a spectacular view of the lake. It is roughly 1 km in length (one-way). The Bruton Farm Hiking Trail branches off the Scorch Lake Lookout Trail and continues for 2.4 km (one-way) to the site of the Bruton Farm. The farm was started in 1875 as a depot to provide food

for area loggers. Today's hikers will see remnants of a farm-house, a barn, and a blacksmith shop. The trail to this site is fairly easy walking with a gradual climb; it passes through a low-lying swampy area and can get muddy.

Algonquin's East Side

The East Side refers to facilities, trails and access points found along the Park road, which stretches 54 km from the Sand Lake Gate to Lake Travers.

- Campground: Achray Campground on Grand Lake offers 39 campsites.
- Interpretive Walking Trails and the Overnight Backpacking Trail: Two day-hiking trails are set up in similar fashion to those on the Highway 60 Corridor. Each has its own informative trail booklet. The 1.5 km Barron Canyon Trail showcases Algonquin's most spectacular scenic wonder, literally taking you to the edge of the 100 m deep gorge. The trail booklet to the 4.5 km Berm Lake Trail discusses the ecology of a typical Algonquin East Side pine forest. Longer hikes are possible as the trail links with the 6 km and 14.8 km loops of the Eastern Pines Backpacking Trail, which also accommodates overnight hiking.
- Horseback Riding: The Lone Creek Horse Trail, opened on an experimental basis in 1999, allows riders to take day rides or to stay overnight at campsites located at the trail head located just off the McManus Lake Access Road (Access Point # 21).
- Interpretive Program: A program of conducted walks, children's activities and nightly theatre presentations runs three or four days a week during July and August. Weekly details are posted on bulletin boards in the Achray Campground.
- The Inside Out Cabin: This cabin was Tom Thomson's home during the summer of 1916 when he worked as a fire ranger. Over the course of the summer, he painted a sign for the cabin, and completed the sketch for *The Jack Pine* (one of his most famous pieces). The Friends of Algonquin Park are currently in the process of constructing interpretive exhibits for the cabin.

The North Side

The North Side is comprised of two separate areas, each can be reached by their own road that branches off Highway 17 between North Bay and Deux Rivers.

- Brent Campground and Day Hiking Trail: The Brent Campground houses 30 sites, an outfitter and supply store. The Brent Crater Interpretive Walking Trail takes hikers to the 2 km wide impact site of an ancient meteorite that crashed 450 million years ago. Four access points are nearby.
- Kiosk Campground: The Kiosk campground contains 17 campsites. Facilities are limited to flush toilets. Two access points are located nearby.

Further Interest:
- The Algonquin Park Information Office distributes a pamphlet entitled *Algonquin South* that describes campsites, day and multi-day canoe routes, trails and winter use.
- Detailed information regarding the East Side's wildlife viewing areas, historical points of interest and short canoe trips can be found in *The Explorer's Guide to Algonquin Park* by Mike Runtz, (Stoddart 1993) - 168 pages
- The free *Algonquin Park Interior Tabloid* has maps and information about facilities, trails and campgrounds on the East and North Side
- Rails have been lifted off the old abandoned railway line that ran through the Park from Kiosk to Achray. Considerable study regarding new development of the area is underway.

17

KEEPING IN TOUCH WITH ALGONQUIN PARK

The Friends of Algonquin Park

Algonquin Park tends to make an impression on its visitors. Many of these people keep abreast of Park happenings by reading *The Raven,* a newsletter published twelve times yearly especially for Park visitors. Each issue deals with a different topic. These are as diverse as unique adaptations of the loon, possible effects of global warming trends on the biodiversity of the Park, historical milestones, special exhibits at the Algonquin Gallery, the latest Algonquin Park books or a detailed account of rare animal attacks. The complete set of twelve *Ravens* is mailed to members of the Friends of Algonquin Park each fall. "The Friends" is a registered charitable organization, which functions to expand and maintain the Park's educational and interpretive program. Its many contributions include the development of over 70 new publications on the Park's history, flora and fauna, and the raising of over one million dollars for use in the construction and staffing of the Visitor Centre and Logging Museum. There are over 3000 members of the Friends of Algonquin Park, many of whom reside outside of Canada. In addition to *The Raven*, members also receive an annual newsletter highlighting the organization's activities over the past year and a catalogue of publications. Members benefit from a 15% discount on items purchased at the Visitor Centre and the Logging Museum, by mail order or through the Internet.

The Friends of Algonquin Park,
P.O. Box 248, Whitney, Ontario, K0J 2M0, (613)-637-2828,
www.algonquinpark.on.ca.

CLIMATE DATA

	J	F	M	A	M	J	J	A	S	O	N	D
Average daily maximum temperature (°C)	-5.3	-3.7	2.4	10.1	17.5	22.3	24.9	23.3	18.6	12.3	4.5	-2.3
Average daily minimum temperature (°C)	-16	-15.1	-9	-1.1	5.4	10.7	13.7	12.9	9	3.2	-2.2	-11.1
Average daily mean temperature (°C)	-10.5	-9.2	-3.2	4.5	11.4	16.6	19.3	18.2	13.9	7.8	1.1	-6.4
Rainfall (mm)	12.9	12	31.5	55.6	74	79.5	73.9	91.7	101.8	87.7	77.1	26.5
Snowfall (cm)	78.9	55.4	32.1	8.7	1.1	0	0	0	0	1.6	29.4	73.5

* The data is for the town of Huntsville which lies approx 43 km west of the Park
* Daily max / mins are calculated within each 24 hour period. The average daily max for the month is the sum of the daily maxs which is then divided by the number of days in the month.
* The average daily mean is the sum of the average daily max and the average daily min divided by two.
* Data compiled by Environment Canada and published in Canadian Climate Normals 1961-1990. Reprinted with permission from the Minister of Public Works and Government Services Canada.

SUN TIMES CHART

Date	Sunrise	Sunset	Length of Day
Jan 1	08:01	16:42 (4:42 pm)	8 hours, 40 min
Jan 15	07:57	16:58 (4:58 pm)	9 hours, 1 min
Feb 1	07:41	17:22 (5:22 pm)	9 hours, 41 min
Feb 15	07:22	17:43 (5:43 pm)	10 hours, 22 min
Mar 1	06:57	18:04 (6:04 pm)	11 hours, 6 min
Mar 15	06:31	18:23 (6:23 pm)	11 hours, 52 min
Apr 1	05:58	18:46 (6:46 pm)	12 hours, 48 min
Apr 15	06:31	20:05 (8:05 pm)	13 hours, 34 min
May 1	06:04	20:26 (8:26 pm)	14 hours, 22 min
May 15	05:45	20:44 (8:44 pm)	14 hours, 59 min
June 1	05:29	21:02 (9:02 pm)	15 hours, 33 min
June 15	05:25	21:11 (9:11 pm)	15 hours, 47 min
July 1	05:29	21:12 (9:12 pm)	15 hours, 45 min
July 15	05:40	21:07 (9:07 pm)	15 hours, 27 min
Aug 1	05:59	20:49 (8:49 pm)	14 hours, 50 min
Aug 15	06:16	20:28 (8:28 pm)	14 hours, 12 min
Sept 1	06:38	19:57 (7:57 pm)	13 hours, 19 min
Sept 15	06:55	19:30 (7:30 pm)	12 hours, 34 min
Oct 1	07:16	18:58 (6:58 pm)	11 hours, 42 min
Oct 15	07:35	18:32 (6:32 pm)	10 hours, 57 min
Nov 1	06:59	17:03 (5:03 pm)	10 hours, 5 min
Nov 15	07:19	16:45 (4:45 pm)	9 hours, 26 min
Dec 1	07:40	16:33 (4:33 pm)	8 hours, 53 min
Dec 15	07:54	16:31 (4:31 pm)	8 hours, 37 min
* sun times vary slightly from year to year			

WILDLIFE SIGHTINGS CHART

Date	Species & Sex	Location	Remarks

WILDLIFE SIGHTINGS CHART

Date	Species & Sex	Location	Remarks

OUTFITTING CHART

OUTFITTER (Highway 60 - Algonquin Park, Dwight, Whitney)	Canoe	Kayak	Bike	Ski	Snow-shoe	Fish tackle	Camping equipment
Algonquin Outfitters: (705) 635-2243 www.algonquinoutfitters.com	RDGS	RDS	RS	R S	R S	S	R S
Portage Store (Alquon Ventures): (705) 633-5622 www.portagestore.com	RDG	R D				S	R S
Opeongo Outfitters: 613-637-5470 1-800-790-1864	RDS	R D	R D			S	R S
Opeongo Algonquin: 613-637-2075 www.algonquinoutfitters.com	RDG	RDG	R D			S	R S
Algonquin Bound: 613-637-5508 www.algonquinbound.com	RDGS	R D				S	R S
East Gate Motel and Outfitters: 613-637-2652 www.mv.net/~outfitters/	RDG				G		R
Bartlett Lodge: 705-633-5543 www.bartlettlodge.com	RG		R				
Swift Canoe and Kayak: (705) 635-1167 www.swiftcanoe.com	S M	S M					
Langford Canoe: 705 766-2447 www.langfordcanoe.com	SMR	S					
Algonquin Wilderness Adv: 905-898-8747 www.algonquin-wilderness.com	G						
Watermark Canoe: 705-766-0970 www.fishnet.on.ca/watermarkcanoe	G						

R = Rentals   **D** = Delivery   **S** = Sales   **G**= Guiding (day or multi-day)   **M** = Manufacturer

DOGSLED GUIDES
Chocpaw Expeditions: (705) 386-0344 www.venturenorth.com/chocpaw
Algonquin Way Kennels: (613) 332-4005 www.mwdesign.net/mush

REMOTE OUTFITTERS & GUIDES: (Not located on Hwy 60)
Kearney, Ontario (Access Point # 2, 3, 4):
Canoe Algonquin: (705) 636-5956 www.canoealgonquin.com
Forest Tower Outfitters: (705) 636-0911

South River, Ontario (Access Point # 1):
Northern Wilderness Outfitters: (705)386-0466 www.northernwilderness.com
Voyageur Outfitting: (705) 386-2813
Canadian Wilderness Trips: (705) 386-2211 www.cdnwildcrncsstrips.com
Chocpaw Expeditions: (705) 386-0344 www.venturenorth.com/chocpaw

Mattawa, Ontario (Access Point # 26, 27, 29):
Algonquin North: (705) 744-3265 www.nordev.com/algonquinnorth
Halfway Chute: (705) 744-2155 www.halfwaychute.com

Brent, Ontario (Access Point # 25, 26, 27)
Brent Outfitting Store: (705) 635-2243 www.algonquinoutfitters.com

Deep River, Ontario (Access Point # 21, 22, 23, 24, 25, 26, 27)
Valley Ventures: (613) 584-2577 www.intranet.ca/~vent

Pembroke, Ontario: (Access Point # 20, 21, 22)
Algonquin Portage: (613) 735-1795 www.algonquinportage.com
Pine Ridge Park & Resort: (613) 732-9891

Madawaska, Ontario: (Acess Point # 16, 17)
Barwick Camp: (613) 637-5541
Riverland Tent and Trailer Camp: (613) 637-5338

Harcourt, Ontario: (Access Point # 15)
Pine Grove Point: (705) 448-2387

Huntsville/ Port Sydney Ontario: (Access Point 2, 3, 4, 5, 6, 7, 8)
Algonquin Outfittcrs: (705) 787-0262 www.algonquinoutfitters.com
Adrienne's Esso Service Centre: (705) 633-5622 www.portagestore.com
Kingfisher Canoe Centre: (705) 385-1148

Gravenhurst. Ontario:
Swift Canoe and Kayak: (705) 687-3710 www.swiftcanoe.com

TRAIL RANKINGS

AVERAGE HIKING TIME & LENGTH OF TRAIL

Centennial Ridges	(6 hours - 10 km)
Mizzy Lake	(5 hours - 11 km)
Track and Tower	(3 3/4 hours - 7.7 km)
Booth's Rock	(3 hours - 5.1 km)
Bat Lake	(2 1/2 hours - 5.6 km)
Hemlock Bluff	(1 1/2 hours - 3.5 km)
Beaver Pond	(1 1/4 hours - 2 km)
Whiskey Rapids	(1 1/4 hours - 2.1 km)
Lookout	(3/4 hours - 1.9 km)
Peck Lake	(3/4 hours - 1.9 km)
Hardwood Lookout	(3/4 hours - 0.8 km)
Two Rivers	(1/2 hour - 2.1 km)
Spruce Bog	(1/2 hour - 1.5km)

DIFFICULTY (most to least)

Centennial Ridges
Track and Tower
Mizzy Lake
Booth's Rock
Lookout
Hardwood Lookout
Beaver Pond
Two Rivers
Bat Lake
Hemlock Bluff
Peck Lake
Whiskey Rapids
Spruce Bog

SCENIC VALUE (best to worst)

Centennial Ridges
Lookout
Booth's Rock
Track and Tower
Two Rivers
Hardwood Lookout
Hemlock Bluff
Bat Lake
Beaver Pond
Peck Lake
Whiskey Rapids
Mizzy Lake
Spruce Bog

WILDLIFE VIEWING (best to worst)
* = good birding area

Mizzy Lake *
Beaver Pond
Spruce Bog *
Track and Tower *
Centennial Ridges
Bat Lake *
Booth's Rock
Hemlock Bluff *
Peck Lake
Whiskey Rapids *
Two Rivers *
Lookout *
Hardwood Lookout *

HIGHWAY 60 CORRIDOR MAP

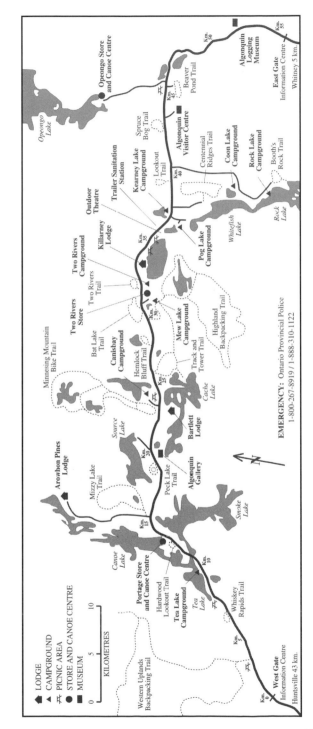

LODGE
CAMPGROUND
PICNIC AREA
STORE AND CANOE CENTRE
MUSEUM

KILOMETRES
0   5   10

Western Uplands
Backpacking Trail

West Gate
Information Centre
Huntsville 43 km.

Km. 0

Km. 5

Whiskey
Rapids Trail

Tea
Lake

**Tea Lake
Campground**

Hardwood
Lookout Trail

**Portage Store
and Canoe Centre**

Canoe
Lake

Km. 10

Km. 15

Mizzy Lake
Trail

**Arowhon Pines
Lodge**

Minnesing Mountain
Bike Trail

Source
Lake

Smoke
Lake

Peck Lake
Trail

**Algonquin
Gallery**

Km. 20

**Bartlett
Lodge**

Cache
Lake

Km. 25

Hemlock
Bluff Trail

**Canisbay
Campground**

Bat Lake
Trail

**Two Rivers
Store**

Track and
Tower Trail

**Mew Lake
Campground**

Highland
Backpacking Trail

Km. 30

Two Rivers
Trail

**Two Rivers
Campground**

**Killarney
Lodge**

Km. 35

**Pog Lake
Campground**

**Outdoor
Theatre**

**Trailer Sanitation
Station**

**Kearney Lake
Campground**

Lookout
Trail

Whitefish
Lake

**Algonquin
Visitor Centre**

Spruce
Bog Trail

Km. 40

Centennial
Ridges Trail

**Coon Lake
Campground**

**Rock Lake
Campground**

Booth's
Rock Trail

Rock
Lake

Km. 45

Beaver
Pond Trail

**Opeongo Store
and Canoe Centre**

Opeongo
Lake

Km. 50

**Algonquin
Logging
Museum**

Km. 55

East Gate
Information Centre
Whitney 5 km.

EMERGENCY: Ontario Provincial Police
1-800-267-8919 / 1-888-310-1122

N

187

Author and Primary Photographer
(pictured on the back cover)

Wayne Van Sickle grew up in the small town of Elmira, Ontario. He studied at the University of Waterloo where he obtained a Bachelor of Mathematics as well as a Bachelor of Arts (Social Development Studies). Frequent travels to out-of-the-way places such as Alaska, Newfoundland, Mozambique and Lesotho have made great impressions on him and the way he looks at life.

He worked for several years in Residential Treatment Centres for disadvantaged youth. In his role as a Child Youth Worker, he made frequent use of the healing aspects of nature and often incorporated outdoor experiences into the treatment plans of the young people he worked with. Several of these youths experienced their first taste of camping on trips lead by Wayne. He brought many of them to Algonquin Park to experience the freedom of a multi-day canoe trip and the thrill of encountering wildlife.

Wayne formed Stonecutter Press in 1997. The name of the publishing house was inspired by an old Chinese story entitled "The Stonecutter". The story encourages people to realize their potential and appreciate their value by looking within themselves. He first read this story in *The Tao of Pooh* - a book about living simply by Benjamin Hoff.

As a full-time self-publisher, Wayne researches, writes, designs, publishes, and promotes his books. He draws frequent support and assistance from his family and friends, each of whom contribute to his work in a wide variety of ways, including visioning, design, photography, motivation, cartography, companionship, inspiration, accounting and tolerance. His ideas of what should be included in a guidebook have been formed by numerous adventures in Canada's national and provincial parks, expeditions to over ten African game parks, visits to the cultural centres of Europe, and by academic studies in the field of tourism.

Wayne is interested in helping charities whose work is aimed at improving situations for our wild places and animals. He has set aside a quantity of books for use as door prizes at charity fundraisers, and is also open to assisting in other ways. Wayne can be reached by email at stonecut@hotmail.com.

Wildlife Photographer

Chris Boettger is an avid canoe tripper and a self-taught wildlife photographer. He was introduced to Algonquin Park at an early age and has extensively explored Algonquin by paddle and portage. Chris has worked in the Park for many years in a variety of positions, including professional canoe guide, and outfitter. His photographs have been exhibited at the Visitor Centre, published in several tourist brochures and on the internet. Chris does most of his photography in Algonquin, but he had also travelled across Canada to photograph Polar Bears in Churchill Manitoba, and the splendor of the Canadian Rockies. He can be reached at email: tripper70@bigfoot.com or website: http://freespirit.cjb.net

Wildlife Photographer

Andrew Mills is a graduate of the School of Photography at Algonquin College in Ottawa. He is currently based in Waterloo, Ontario and works as both a wedding photographer and a free lance wildlife photographer. Andrew makes frequent trips to Algonquin Park in each of the four seasons. Recently, while on a trip to Mount Robson Provincial Park in British Columbia he had the unpleasant experience of watching his Nikon camera system and his tripod topple over a waterfall. He claims that camera insurance was the best purchase he ever made! His online gallery can be visited at http://home.golden.net/~toad.

Cartography

Valdis Kalnins is an accomplished international adventurer and has toured much of northern Ontario by canoe. He holds a Masters degree in Environmental Studies from the University of Waterloo and currently resides in Kalamazoo, Michigan. When he is not busy working or travelling, Valdis exercises his cartographic skills by designing customized maps for various publications. His email address is the_mapmaker@hotmail.com.

ASPEN VALLEY WILDLIFFE SANCTUARY
(Rosseau, Ontario)

Aspen Valley has been in operation for over 25 years. It is located on 700 acres of land. The Sanctuary's mandate is to take in sick, injured or orphaned animals, nurse them to health and release them into their natural habitat. A portion of the proceeds from the sale of this book will be donated to the Sanctuary.

The Sanctuary looks after a variety of mammals including raccoons, foxes, skunks, beavers and wolves. The animals arrive from as close as a few miles down the road, to as far away as the other side of the continent. One orphaned timber wolf was flown by executive jet from Ungava Bay on the border of Labrador and Northern Quebec. Orphaned black bear cubs hibernate each winter in naturalized enclosures before being released the following spring. Naturalized areas help to stimulate the survival instincts that allow the creatures to function properly when released back into the wild. A special six-acre moose enclosure was originally built around a pond for a young moose that was abandoned by its mother when it became trapped under a cottage dock in Northern Ontario. Tony Grant, the Sanctuary's manger fed it a lamb's-milk substitute every two hours for several months.

Staff and volunteers work closely with veterinarians, biologists and other experts. An educational program, which promotes man's ability to live in harmony with nature, runs out of an old barn on the premises. It attracts schools and other groups.

The Wildlife Sanctuary is a registered charity and runs exclusively on personal and corporate donations. The majority of donations go toward the cost of feeding the animals (over $75,000 per year)!

Donations or queries should be directed to:
The Aspen Valley Wildlife Sanctuary, General Delivery, Rosseau, Ont., Box 183, P0C 1J0, Tel: (705) 732-6368

The Sanctuary is just over an hour's drive from Algonquin Park's West Gate. It is open to the public Wed and Sun (12 – 4 p.m.)
Directions: Exit Highway 11 at Muskoka Road 3 (Huntsville's most southern exit). Travel west for roughly 30 km, then turn left onto Crawford Street. The Sanctuary's barn appears on the right a few km later.

BIBLIOGRAPHY

(In addition to the publications listed throughout the book in the further interest sections)

Addison, Ottelyn. *Tom Thomson: the Algonquin Years*. Toronto: McGraw-Hill Ryerson Limited, 1975.

Bateman, Robert. *The Art of Robert Bateman*. Toronto: Madison Books, 1981.

Burt, William, H. *A Field Guide to Mammals*. Boston: Houghton Mifflin Company, 1976.

Chapman, Joseph, A & Feldhamer, George, A. *Wild Mammals of North America*. Baltimore: The John's Hopkins University Press, 1982.

Crosskey, Roger. W. *The Natural History of Blackflies*. New York: John Wiley & Sons, 1993.

Farrar, John Laird. *Trees in Canada*. Markham: Fitzhenry & Whiteside Limited, 1995.

Godfrey, W. Earl, *The Birds of Canada*. Ottawa: Queens Printer, 1966.

Hayton, A. *The Age Structure and Population Dynamics of Some Black Flies in Algonquin Park, Ontario*. M. Sc. Thesis, University of Waterloo, Waterloo, Ontario 1979.

Hill, Charles C. *The Group of Seven: Art for a Nation*. Toronto: McClelland & Steward Inc., 1995.

Hunter, Fiona. Personal Communication, May 1999.

Kim, Ke. C. *Black Flies: Ecology, Population Management, and Annotated World List*, The Pennsylvania State University, 1987.

Kricher, John C. & Morrison, Gordon. *Ecology of Eastern Forests*. Boston: Houghton Mifflin Company, 1988.

Mellen, Peter. *The Group of Seven*. Toronto: McClelland & Steward Inc., 1976.

Murray, Joan. *Northern Lights: Masterpieces of Tom Thomson and the Group of Seven*. Toronto: Key Porter Books Limited, 1994.

Murray, Joan. *The Best of the Group of Seven*. Toronto: McClelland & Steward Inc., 1993.

Nowak, Ronald, M & Paradiso, John, L. *Walker's Mammals of the World*. Baltimore: The John Hopkins University Press, 1983.

Peterson, Roger, T. *A Field Guide to the Birds of Eastern and Central North America*. Boston: Houghton Mifflin Company, 1980.

Pimlott D.H. et al. *The Ecology of the Timber Wolf in Alonquin Provincial Park*. (Fish and Wildlife Research Branch Report No 87) Ontario Ministry of Natural Resources, 1977.

Strickland, D. *Juvenile Dispersal in Gray Jay; Dominant Brood Member Expels Siblings from Natal Territory*. Canadian Journal of Zoology, 69:2935-2945.

Strickland, D. *Finding (and Watching) Gray Jays in Algonquin Park*.
Ontario Birds, 10: 1-10.

Strickland, D.& H. Ouellet. "Gray Jay" in *The Birds of North America*,
No. 40, editors: A. Poole, P. Stettenheim, F. Gill. Philadelphia: The
Academy of Natural Sciences, 1993

Strickland, D. *Bat Lake Trail: Basic Algonquin Ecology*. Whitney: The
Friends of Algonquin Park, 1992.

Strickland, D. *Beaver Pond Trail: Algonquin Beaver Ecology*. Whitney:
The Friends of Algonquin Park, 1995.

Strickland, D. *Booth's Rock Hiking Trail: Man and the Algonquin
Environment*. Whitney: The Friends of Algonquin Park, 1994.

Strickland, D. *Centennial Ridges Trail: Historical Figures of Algonquin
Park*. Whitney: The Friends of Algonquin Park, 1993.

Strickland, D. *Hardwood Lookout Trail: Algonquin Hardwood Forest
Ecology*. Whitney: The Friends of Algonquin Park, 1994.

Strickland, D. *Hemlock Bluff Trail: Research in Algonquin..* Whitney:
The Friends of Algonquin Park, 1991.

Strickland, D. *Lookout Trail: Algonquin Geology*. Whitney: The Friends
of Algonquin Park, 1996.

Strickland, D. *Mizzy Lake Trail: Wildlife in Algonquin*. Whitney: The
Friends of Algonquin Park, 1993.

Strickland, D. *Peck Lake Trail: Ecology of an Algonquin Lake*. Whitney:
The Friends of Algonquin Park, 1992.

Strickland, D. *Spruce Bog Boardwalk: Algonquin Spruce Bog Ecology*.
Whitney: The Friends of Algonquin Park, 1993.

Strickland, D. *Two Rivers Trail: Changes in Algonquin Forests*.
Whitney: The Friends of Algonquin Park, 1991.

Strickland, D. *Track and Tower Trail: A Look into Algonquin's Past*.
Whitney: The Friends of Algonquin Park, 1992.

Strickland, D. *Whiskey Rapids Trail: Algonquin River Ecology*.
Whitney: The Friends of Algonquin Park, 1992

Tozer, R. *Checklist and Seasonal Status of the Birds of Algonquin
Provincial Park*. Whitney: The Friends of Algonquin Park, 1990.

NOTES

NOTES

GUIDE BOOK ORDER FORM

Algonquin Park Visitor's Guide

A comprehensive introduction to the wildlife, trails, nature, activities, services, history and art of Algonquin Provincial Park. Over 80 photographs, maps and charts compliment the text which is designed to helps readers plan their visit, appreciate Park surroundings and recollect their adventures for years to come.
200 pages, English, by Wayne Van Sickle, ISBN# 0-9684005-1-5

$18.95 Cdn   (+ Shipping and Handling)

Naturparkführer Algonquin Park Kanada

A comprehensive introduction to the wildlife, trails, nature, activities, services and history of Algonquin Provincial Park. Over 80 photographs, maps and charts compliment the text which is designed to helps readers plan their visit, appreciate Park surroundings and recollect their adventures for years to come. Entirely in the German language.
208 pages, German, by Wayne Van Sickle, ISBN# 0-9684005-0-7

$19.95 Cdn   (+ Shipping and Handling)

Order by mail
Send a cheque or money order
(in Canadian Funds) to:
Stonecutter Press
212 Arthur Street South
Elmira, Ontario, Canada
N3B 2P1

Shipping and Handling fees
(for 1 book):
Canada: $2.00
USA: $5.00
Europe & elsewhere: $8.00
 Canadian residents add $1.33 GST

Order through our website
Visit www.algonquinbooks.cjb.net and order a signed copy mailed
directly to your home.

Order by E-mail
Send an E-mail to stonecut@hotmail.com and you will receive an order
form by return E-mail.

EMERGENCIES

In case of emergency anywhere in Ontario, including Algonquin Provincial Park, the Ontario Provincial Police (O.P.P.) are available 24 hours a day, 365 days a year. They manage all types of emergencies including medical, fire, theft and automobile. They can be reached at either 1-800-267-8919 or 1-888-310-1122. These numbers can be dialed free of charge from any telephone, including telephone booths.

24 Hour Automobile Service and Towing
- Whitney, Ontario: Mochulla Auto Service: (613) 637-2752
- Dwight, Ontario: Pretty's Towing: 1-800-410-7114
- Huntsville, Ontario: Edward's Towing: (705) 789-6384
- South River, Ontario: John Beddard (705) 386-0759
- Mattawa, Ontario: Full Line Auto (705) 744-1500
- Deep River, Ontario: Gasman Towing: (613) 584-3136
- Pembroke, Ontario: Marcel's Towing: (613) 735-0987